S0-AHB-366

Nothing Works But Everything Works Out

Nothing Works But Everything Works Out

My Peace Corps Experience in the West Region of Cameroon

Leigh Marie Dannhauser

This book is based off of my own memories and thoughts. It does not reflect the position of the United States Peace Corps or the United States Government.

Copyright © 2019 by Leigh Marie Dannhauser

All rights reserved. No part of this book may be used or reproduced in any manner whatsoever without written permission, except in the case of brief quotations embodied in critical articles and reviews. For information address Leigh Marie Dannhauser at leigh.dannhauser@gmail.com.

ISBN (Print) 978-1-7333540-0-4

ISBN (Ebook) 978-1-7333540-1-1

Cover design by Klassic Designs.

Front cover photo by Leigh Marie Dannhauser. Back cover photos by Abigail Koscik and Frances Vasquez.

Printed in the United States of America.

In memory of my Good Old Mom, Sandy Dannhauser

GOM, as she signed every note or postcard to me and my siblings, gave me the motivation to quit my well-paying office job to volunteer in a rural village in Cameroon for two years. Her strength and her generosity were something I didn't quite understand while I was younger, but I now know that she is and always will be the strongest person I've ever met.

Author's Note

It is important to note that everybody's Peace Corps experience is different. This is mine. It will not be the same as the experience of your friend or family member, or your experience if you have been or will be a Peace Corps Volunteer. There are parallels but over 235,000 volunteers have served in countries around the world since President John F. Kennedy started the program in 1961, and we all have our own unique stories to tell.

1

"Nothing works but everything works out" is one of the sayings we had in Peace Corps Cameroon. It is a pretty straightforward saying. As volunteers we would try to make plans, and of course those plans never worked. But the goals of the plans, sometimes adapted to new circumstances, were usually achieved. It could have to do with a project, a travel day – basically any aspect of service. It almost never worked as planned, but it would work out in the end. The same is true of my service, from even before I left the United States.

I decided in August 2016 that I wanted to join the Peace Corps. I had many doubts before telling my dad that I wanted to do it. I had been living about two hours from home for a little over a year at that point and was visiting every weekend. I had a job that I was good at and paid well, even if I didn't love it. I had finally gotten through the hardest part of my life to date after dealing with the death of my mom and having major elbow surgery. Why would I throw away all of that comfort to make such a huge change?

I didn't think that I had answered those questions before I started the conversation with my dad. My dad isn't one who says yes or no right away to a crazy idea. He is someone who asks questions to help me see a situation with a fresh perspective. Through his supportive questions I was able to realize that I was not looking to run away from that year's troubles. It was not a crisis of a desperate need to change. It was not that I didn't feel deserving of my job or living close to home.

I realized that I simply wanted to give back. I have been fortunate in my life. I was living in the United States, had a great education at two renowned institutions, and most importantly had a family that loved and supported me no matter what I did. That is rare in the world as a whole. I felt, and still feel, that people should give back in whatever ways that they can, something that was heavily influenced by my mother. For me, joining the Peace Corps and spending over two years integrated in a foreign community was the best way to make a difference, and that is exactly what I told my dad during that conversation.

Applicants to the Peace Corps can either apply to specific countries or let the Peace Corps send them where they are needed most. My dad was not thrilled at first when I told him I was applying to serve anywhere the Peace Corps chose to send me. He was concerned about it from a safety perspective, but I viewed it as the best way to make a difference. To me, choosing where I would be serving when I had no idea about the needs of those countries would undercut the impact I was hoping to make. I felt that the way to make the biggest impact would be to let the Peace Corps decide what the needs of each country were, compare it to my application and resume, and decide where to send me.

Soon after I completed the application in September 2016, I got an email saying I was being considered as a business advising volunteer for Peru leaving in April 2017. I had my interview the following week, and within a month I had gotten my acceptance for Peace Corps Peru. I started learning Spanish, studying Peruvian economics, and planning my trips throughout the country. I quit my job in January 2017 and by March was in the process of moving out of my apartment.

To put it simply, I was a stressed-out mess. I was grasping at straws for things to worry about, even though I was very well prepared and I knew it. One morning I saw a story in the New York Times about storms that ravaged Peru and caused mudslides. I told my twin sister, Casey, that I was worried it could affect my service there. She told me I was crazy and that as usual I was just looking for things to worry about.

Not even eight hours later I was sitting in a recliner in my living room when I got a phone call saying I was no longer going to Peru to serve as a business advising volunteer. There was a lot of flood and mudslide damage throughout the country, forcing them to cancel my volunteer group. Then they asked if I would be open to be serving in another country with a departure date before October. When I said yes, they told me it would take them about three weeks to find me a new placement. I can admit now that after the call ended, I broke down in that recliner while my dad and my sister comforted me. In those first moments it felt like my service had crumbled around me before it even began. I wasn't getting the opportunity to complete the work that I had already spent significant time preparing for.

But soon after, I was okay. I realized that my service was not dependent on Peru. I had not applied to Peru. I was prepared to serve there, but I could just as easily prepare for service somewhere else. After all, I would still be able to serve somewhere. While I did not know it then, my quick turnaround about such a big blow started to prepare me to deal with the ups and downs of a Peace Corps service. I was already learning that while things don't work as planned, they eventually work out. The difference for me was that I hadn't actually left the United States yet. Instead of spending the three weeks wallowing in disappointment that I was not going to Peru anymore, I spent it being the control freak that I had always been, trying to predict where I would be going and when. Given that I had told the Peace Corps to put me anywhere and do anything, an impressive move for a self-described control freak, it was an impossible task. I made my brother, sister, and dad sit around a table, and we each took turns choosing a country from a list I created of countries with departure dates for business advising volunteers soon after my original departure. It was like a fantasy football draft except this was an attempt to choose the winner instead of putting together the best team, and this one didn't have creative team names.

I should have known that it wouldn't be that easy.

A little under three weeks later, I was back in Arlington, Massachusetts moving the last boxes from my apartment in preparation for the moving truck to take my furniture to my dad's basement on Cape Cod. After all, I had gotten out of my lease early in preparation of moving to Peru. As I was driving down Massachusetts Avenue in the pouring rain, I got my phone call from the Peace Corps. I pulled over was offered a spot in Cameroon to serve as a health extension volunteer. I had three days to accept the offer. Clearly my assumption for still being a business advising volunteer had been wrong, but I knew before I even hung up the phone with the recruiter that I would be taking the position.

My dad, on the other hand, was not as immediately thrilled. He was supportive of my decision since I am an adult and he knew that he couldn't change my mind. However, in his mind he was comparing the position of a health extension volunteer in Cameroon with a business advising volunteer in Peru in terms of both safety and my career. He thought that Peru would be safer. I am not sure why but I can only assume it felt safer being that much closer and being in the same time zone. He did have a point in terms of my career, but I knew that my joining the Peace Corps had nothing to do with that. The difference between our reactions stems from from this: I was thinking about it from the perspective of wanting to serve wherever they needed me while he was comparing it to something that I would never get- the role in Peru. He came around quickly with Casey's help, and I spent the following four months trying to learn French and preparing for a life in Cameroon.

At this point you might be confused. After all, I spent my 27 months as an agriculture volunteer instead of a health extension volunteer. Well, as I mentioned, my Peace Corps service was filled with lessons showing me that I cannot control everything. Learning that things can change at the last moment was one of those lessons.

Fast-forward to September. I arrived in Cameroon after a two-day staging event in Philadelphia. I had made it and was about to start my life as a health extension volunteer. I didn't get a call three weeks before departure like I had for Peru, so I felt confident that I had everything under control. The facade of control did not last even 12 hours in Cameroon. During our dinner soon after we landed in Cameroon, we had to take our training schedules. Health and agriculture volunteers arrive together in Cameroon and are assigned different colored folders to make schedule distribution easier. That night, they were missing a health folder and had an extra agriculture folder. You can likely guess who had the wrong folder.

During our first session the following morning, I got pulled aside by the volunteer greeters assigned to help us during our first week. I will never forget that conversation, opening with the question of why I took the health calendar of training events. I was told that while everything I had gotten from headquarters said I was a health volunteer, in the Cameroon system I was listed as an agriculture volunteer. They asked me if I would be willing to switch work sectors. It seemed like they were in a bind. They needed an agriculture volunteer, and apparently I was supposed to be one. At this point I had a choice to make. I could have insisted on staying a health volunteer. But the Peace Corps in Cameroon knows what their country needs. Without hesitation, I chose to switch, admitting that I didn't have any experience in either field anyway.

Just like that, I became an agriculture volunteer. I had changed countries twice and sectors three times and I was still on Day 1. But that willingness to be flexible shaped my service and my experiences, and it is quite possible that I would have no experiences to write about had I not chosen to be flexible from the very beginning. My application could have been denied to a specific country, I could have been denied had I decided to apply to specifically Peru again, and I do not even want to think about what would have happened to me had I demanded I stay a health volunteer. Throughout my service I thought back on these moments when I needed a reminder to be flexible. It was tough to do even until the very end of my service. But when I stopped trying to control every facet of life and took a second to breathe, things simply went smoother. That is not to say that they went perfectly, and I eventually learned to be okay with that as well. After all, even when nothing was working I trusted that it would all work out.

2

I will say it until I'm blue in the face that you cannot compare someone's Peace Corps service to anyone else's. With that being said, the 2017 Agriculture stage (what a group of trainees who start together are called) in Cameroon likely had one of the most unique starts to service. For us, the first few days seemed to be normal. After the blur of staging in Philadelphia and over 24 hours of traveling to get to Yaoundé (the capital of Cameroon), we arrived safely and not too much the worse for wear. As was typical for the new training stages, we stayed in the capital city for two or three days to do more paperwork, take language tests, and have a medical check-up. On the last evening in the capital, we were treated to the customary Cameroon trainee dinner at the country director's house. The following day the agriculture and health volunteers were to load up onto different buses since we were going to different training villages. The agriculture group was to go to a village called

Mbengwi in the North West region for a month, learning the more technical aspects of farming in Cameroon before heading to Foumbot, a village in the West region, where the health group was to spend the full ten weeks.

That dinner was the last "normal" experience for the agriculture stage for the next month, if you believe in such a thing as a normal Peace Corps experience. The country director announced that the agriculture group would no longer be going to Mbengwi the next day; we would instead spend a few more days at the hotel in Yaoundé.

A bit of history: At the time we arrived in Cameroon, a crisis was deepening in the North West and South West regions — the Anglophone sections of the country. When Germany lost World War I, the colony was split between the French and the English. When the English colony gained independence, its leaders were given a choice. They could vote to join the newly independent Cameroon or Nigeria. The northern part of the colony chose to join Nigeria while the southern part of the colony chose to join Cameroon, with an understanding that they would have their own government. The result, still in effect today, was two distinct parts of the new country — the Francophone regions that had been part of the French colony and the Anglophone regions that had been part of the English colony.

To put it almost too simply, many in the Anglophone regions were protesting the concentration of power in the Francophone regions, since over the decades since the unification the government in Yaoundé had been taking away the rights originally agreed upon. Many, including militant groups, were calling for secession and the creation of a new country called Ambazonia. When we arrived in Cameroon in 2017, the crisis had been going on for a few years at that point, including internet shutdowns for the regions and clashes between protestors and police, but now the violence was escalating. It was decided that the crisis was getting too intense for volunteers to continue to live and work safely in the regions. As a result, those volunteers already in the Anglophone regions were evacuated while we sat in the hotel in Yaoundé.

With civil unrest escalating, there were not a lot of options for the agriculture group for our ten week training program. We couldn't go anywhere in the Anglophone regions due to the protests. We couldn't go to Foumbot because our host families were not yet ready for our arrival. It was not as simple as picking a new training farm in the Francophone regions, because none were available on such short notice. We did visit one training farm in the South region, but it was just for a day to give us a brief introduction. Another day, to get us out of the hotel we were essentially sequestered in while the staff worked to figure out what to do with the 20 of us, we went to the Mafou Primate Park. At the same time, the programming team was working to figure out what on earth to do with the volunteers who had been evacuated from the North West and South West regions. They were swamped. But within three days they had found a solution for us. After a week in Cameroon, we hopped on a bus headed to the village of Banganté in the West region.

We left one hotel for another. We arrived in Banganté at the APADER Training Farm but there was nowhere for us to stay. Ordinarily during this training period volunteers stay with host families, but, there was no time for the programing team to set those up. We trainees at that point were just along for the ride. We ended up staying in a hotel near the training farm for two nights. The training farm employees turned some old stables into dorms for us in record time. The rooms were tiny, probably 10 feet across by 15 feet long. The vast majority of the space in the rooms was taken up by two bunk beds — the rest of the space was taken up by all of the baggage that the four volunteers per room had packed for the next two years. In the back of each room was a little stall with a bucket flush toilet and a small curtain serving as a door. Behind the row of dorms was a series of latrines for us to bathe in. Our trainings, breakfasts, and lunches were held in the classroom at the top of the hill, not even 50 yards away from the dorms.

It was not a normal situation, but it quickly became normal for us. There were some downsides to our isolated dorm lifestyle, such as not being forced to practice French in the evenings and not learning much culture outside of the training sessions. Additionally, for dinner we had to fend for ourselves. We had no kitchen and had to hop on motos to ride to the center of Banganté in order to eat. Through all of that, we managed it. More than that, I would like to think we thrived. One of the benefits of our crazy situation was that we were introduced to life in Cameroon very slowly. We were not going to a host family's house just after a few days in country with barely any language skills. We got to get to know each other a lot better, too, since we weren't scattered in village quarters that could be over a 45 minute walk from the training center. After getting back from the center of Banganté, we spent our evenings watching movies on people's computers, studying, reading, or playing cards.

After about a month, we were on our way to Foumbot for the second half of our training. Things got more normal, and we stayed with host families while we continued our training program. After that, the main difference between our experience and those of other training stages was when we learned about out sites. Trainees typically learn where they will live before the halfway point of training, and then spend a week visiting a current volunteer at a site near where the trainee will be placed. But we didn't find out until our eighth week of training Why? It went back to the Anglophone crisis. Out of the 20 agriculture trainees, 12 of us were supposed to be going to the North West or South West regions. That had been the program focus area, so that strategy had to be adapted. The staff, after sorting out what to do with the new trainees sitting in a Yaoundé hotel, had to find a large number of new sites for both those evacuated and the soon to be volunteers. The staff did an incredible job under time pressure, finally finding us sites and telling us in a small ceremony. This was weeks later than usual, but at that point we had already learned that it was not something we could control and that no matter how many times we asked, we would not be told before they were ready to tell us.

Looking back, I realize we were already learning to adapt. Back then, we felt like we didn't have a choice. We didn't have the option of going to Mbengwi, and nothing we did could change that. We made the best out of the situation and were flexible. I think that somehow we were already learning the mantra that things never work out the way they are planned, but they almost always work out eventually. I'm glad we got that lesson so early. It was important to learn that there is no base level of smoothness to life in the Peace Corps, and that was something we experienced first hand before we were even living on our own.

3

My first real introduction to life in Cameroon was my time with my homestay family in the last few weeks of training. Peace Corps trainees live with homestay families, the idea being that it helps with a broad range of aspects of the cultural divide including but not limited to language, food, and customs. In many Peace Corps countries volunteers live with families for the entirety of their service but in Cameroon that is not the case. I lived with mine for just five weeks. My homestay dad was in Douala, the port city of Cameroon, for the vast majority of my time there, so much time in fact that I never properly learned his name. He was just saved in my phone as "Host Dad." I lived in a concession with his fiancé Fortune, their two children Rayan and Amira who were both in primary school, and their house girl Martine who was in high school. Our training village was a place where a girl could live and work for a family not her own in return for being fed and her schooling being paid for. Oftentimes this work was cooking, cleaning, and helping take care of the household children, which during my stay with them included me.

My concession's setup was unique. Almost every other agriculture volunteer lived in a single building shared with the entire family. My homestay, however, was divided up into four buildings. One was a big house under construction. Martine, Amira, and Rayan slept on mattresses on the floor of one of it's unfinished rooms. The next building over was long and thin with a patio in the middle. The patio was split down the middle with a wall, and there were doors on either side. The layout on either side of the wall, which continued through the building, mirrored one another. There was a small living room that was walked through to get to a bedroom. One side was treated as the master suite, and I lived in what could be called a mother-in-law suite on the other side. My living room served as a makeshift kitchen as well. The other two buildings were much smaller and made of mud brick. The first was at the end of the alley between the two larger cement buildings. It was a simple square hut that served as the outdoor kitchen. A few feet away, behind the building with the suites, was the pit latrine. It was a setup I had never seen before and I will likely never see again, but it was my new home.

There are some parts of my homestay that all blurred together after over two years and others that stick out to me as if they happened yesterday. One of those that stands out was our grand arrival and moving in after spending a month living in the cramped dorms in Banganté. When we arrived, we were all brought to the training center, where members of our host families were waiting for us. We then had a quick ceremony matching trainee with family. Hasty introductions were made before the host family helped get the trainee's bags into the Peace Corps car that would help bring all of our stuff to our homestay houses. Keep in mind that at that point we were lugging the bags we packed for our two years of service plus everything we had accumulated thus far at training, like medical kits and too many handbooks to count.

When my name was called, Fortune and her son Rayan stood up while all of the other remaining host families and trainees applauded. Fortune gave me a big welcome hug while Rayan stared at me. I couldn't really blame him. He was surrounded by more white people than he had ever seen in his young life. Fortune handed him my moto helmet to carry, which he immediately put onto his head as he climbed into the car. As we were dropping other families and trainees off, Fortune asked me if it was okay if I was called "Tante," (she pronounced it tahn-tee) or aunt in French. I said of course. She turned to her son and said something along the lines of "Rayan, we will call her Tante Leg." Leigh is a very difficult name for Cameroonians to pronounce when they see it spelled like that, and Fortune is not the only person to think "leg" is the proper pronunciation. Any Cameroonian who read my name to confirm my identity thought my name was Leg Mary instead of Leigh Marie. I could already tell that Fortune was a force to be reckoned with, a fierce younger woman whose bad side you'd never want to get on. It didn't help that at that point I was timid, tired from the long bus ride from Banganté, and still didn't know much French. I didn't bother to correct her and I was always known to my homestay family as Tante Leg. It would never fail to put a smile on my face as Rayan, his sister Amira, and all of the neighborhood children would yell, "Tante Leg! Tante Leg!" when I would return home after yet another long day at training.

One of the first culture lessons I learned living with Fortune was the importance of having clean shoes. We woke up early my first morning to give us time for her to walk me to the training center, basically making sure her white girl didn't get lost on the way. When we both walked into the alleyway to head over, she stopped me and yelled at me about my shoes. Why? They were too dirty. I hadn't washed them since arriving in Cameroon because I didn't know the cultural importance. She made me take them off and showed me the proper way of cleaning them with a scrub brush, saying that from now on I was to do it and that I was to do it every morning before I left the concession. My first impressions of my host mother were spot on. It took just a few minutes and off we went. Since it was a Saturday, we only had a half day of training that ended up being just a quick meeting about how our first nights went and us trainees discussing how happy we all were to see one another after our first night apart in over a month. From there I walked back to the concession to meet Fortune to head to the market with her. She took one look at my shoes and made me wash them again before we left. They barely got any dirt on them on the walk to and from the training center, but they weren't clean enough. When we got back from the market, I had to clean them a third time because she didn't want me leaving in the morning forgetting to clean them. She said that if I left the house with dirty shoes, it would affect her reputation since she was responsible for me, and it would say that she was the type of mother that allowed her children outside when they weren't proper. From then on I probably had the cleanest shoes of all of the trainees every day, although I'll admit that didn't last too long after I arrived at site.

Eventually, life became routine. I would get up early and make myself a two-egg omelet. Fortune showed me on my first morning and then said that I was expected to do it, exactly the way she showed me, for myself from then on out. I learned that she was very big on making sure that I was self-reliant and that I helped around the concession. Before leaving each day, I was to wash my dishes and help Amira and Martine with the morning chores. One of those was sweeping the alley, which confused me at first because it was a gravel alleyway. It was not unique to my homestay, as I saw it all over — people sweeping the dirt in front of their houses with bunched together straw to make it proper. By giving me responsibilities, Fortune was making sure that I would be able to fend for myself when I was no longer in her care. Then I would walk Amira and Rayan to their school, which was on the way to my training center. I created a handshake with them, basically just a high five and a finger snap. It was simple but it made the other kids jealous that they had a handshake with one of the white people in town.

Training was full nine hour days five days a week, and four additional hours on Saturdays. Afterwards most trainees didn't go straight home, instead either continuing to hang out at the training center, heading to town, or to a local bar. Although our curfew wasn't until 7:00 p.m. I would always be home by 6:00 p.m. to watch the *Santa Diablo* soap opera with Martine, Amira, and Rayan. If I came home right before 6:00 p.m. they would tell me to hurry up to collect my water and bathe because I couldn't miss a minute of it. They would yell, "Santa Diablo! Santa Diablo!" if I came home too close to showtime. Afterwards, Martine would serve us dinner and then we would sit for awhile together usually doing our respective work. Martine and the kids would be doing homework while I would be either working on a practice presentation or practicing my French grammar for our next language proficiency interview. Sometimes we would continue watching TV together. If the power was out then we would eat outside, sitting crosslegged on the patio with our plates in our lap and the moon serving as our light. We would all then just go to bed since there really wasn't anything else we could do in the dark.

This routine would only differ for two reasons — if it my host dad was home or if it was a weekend. If he was there then Martine, Amira, and I would have to eat in the living room/kitchen with the ripped furniture off of my room while Fortune and Rayan joined him for dinner in the living room with the nice furniture and the TV. I was never able to figure out why that was the case since nobody else had ever heard of that before, and I didn't think it was my place to ask my homestay family such a question. On weekends I would try to take a trip to market and/or relax in my room, taking time to be in my own space. Personal space was difficult to find since I was always surrounded by either other trainees or my host family, and even if I was in my room on a Saturday afternoon Rayan and the neighborhood kids would yell for me to come play with them.

Sundays were our only day off of of training, but that didn't mean that there wasn't work to be done. It was our only free day for laundry. The hardest part of doing laundry while living with my homestay family was collecting water. While the concessions of most other agriculture trainees had wells in them, mine was 50 yards away uphill. I would have to try to not spill, fall, or both on my way back down to the house, and on Sundays I would always have an audience. On my third Sunday of doing laundry I saw Amira disappear behind one of the buildings and come back with a bucket full of water. I was confused, since Fortune made it very clear on the tour where the well was. Since I was told our well was much further away I decided to borrow two 20 liter water jugs from the Peace Corps to decrease how many trips to the well I had to make. I didn't realize how heavy they would be when full as I confidently carried my two new water jugs up to the well to fill them. Once filled I quickly realized I couldn't actually carry them both back down on my own. I could barely lift even one. One of the neighbors saw me trying to figure out what on earth I was going to do and lent a hand. With ease she put one of the jugs on her head while she carried her own big bucket with her hand. I, on the other hand, struggled to carry the one water jug with two hands, trying not to trip over it as I waddled downhill with dangling between my legs. It was a humbling experience and afterwards I made sure to only bring one water jug with me at a time. Once I saw Amira get water from the magically appearing concession well, however, collecting water became less of an issue.

Towards the end of homestay, trainees were expected to step a little bit outside of their routine, including cooking a dish from home for their new family. This posed some challenges for me. First, I am a terrible cook. Second, I was afraid of their stove top. It was one of those stovetops that had to be lit manually after turning the gas on. Fortune and Martine would laugh at me as I would do it in the wrong order, not knowing any better and not being corrected. I would turn the gas on, light the match, and throw it into the stovetop to avoid burning my hand. More often than not, the match would blow out in my effort to toss it into the leaking gas. I decided to face my fears and go with one of my strengths – breakfast for dinner. I bought a loaf of sugar bread from the bakery in the center of town and a bunch of eggs. That night I made them French toast and scrambled eggs, neither of which was something that anyone in the family had tried before. Martine even watched over as I made the French toast, eager to learn. I don't think they liked either very much, and were very confused by the scrambled eggs since all eggs in Cameroon are beaten and fried into what they call an omelette, even if there is nothing in it. Still, it was a fun experience to attempt to share some of my favorite foods with them, and they claimed to like it and did eat all of it.

Living with Fortune, Martine, Amira, and Rayan was an eye-opening experience. At times I wished that I could have stayed with them longer, since we were just getting used to one another by the time I had to leave. On the other hand, I probably would have gotten antsy since I am someone who desperately needs time to herself on a much more regular basis. Either way, I was sad to leave. I brought them gifts from the United States, which I gave a few nights before I left. Martine and Amira got nail polish, and they immediately laid down on one of the patios painting their nails. I gave Fortune a longer lasting gift in the form of a Cape Cod shirt, something that she could wear and be reminded of her first white daughter. Of course I didn't know when I bought the shirt that white is a terrible idea given all of the dust and mud that is a part of living in Cameroon. When I handed Fortune the shirt, Rayan loudly exclaimed in French, "But it's white!" Fortune quickly shushed him and thanked me for the gift. Rayan got a tennis ball, which was actually an on the spot gift. I didn't think about having a younger host brother and as such I didn't bring anything suitable. I did bring a tennis ball, mostly for rolling out stiff muscles. I searched through the bags that I never truly unpacked for something suitable and the tennis ball was the only thing I could find. Rayan loved it, as did Amira. For my last few nights after eating, I would sit in a chair in the alley tossing the ball towards one of them who was using a small, handheld chalkboard as a bat. The other would get the ball and give it to me before taking their turn. We would usually play until Fortune told them that they had to do their schoolwork.

When I think of my homestay, these are the memories that come back to me. It isn't the great food. It isn't all of the work that I had to do as a trainee. It is the experiences that I had with the people, for better or worse. They were my first family in Cameroon and they took me under their wing, showing me the ropes to prepare me to survive in a village on my own. I came back a week after leaving to attend Fortune and my host dad's wedding, and then again a year later. I was always welcomed back with a big hug serving to remind me that while I lived there barely more than a month, I would always be a part of their family.

4

After ten weeks of training, it was time for us to be sworn
in as volunteers. We learned how to map farms, dig proper
garden beds with village materials, and do a community
needs assessment. We had improved our ability to speak
French, learned about aspects of general Cameroon culture,
and so much more. We had passed our language and
technical tests. We had earned the title of volunteer. All that
was left was our ceremony.

It is tradition in Peace Corps Cameroon for all of the
trainees to wear matching pagne to the ceremony. Pagne is
fabric of beautiful patterns that Cameroonians buy in either
three meters or six meters before taking it to a tailor to have
it the fabric turned into clothes. In villages, this is what most
women wear in the form of long dresses that can be worn
on the farm, to the market, and to ceremonies. They use it
to wrap pots of food or cultivated beans to make them easier
to carry on their heads. Mothers have extra pieces that they

use to wrap around themselves to hold their babies on their backs. You would only be able to see little feet sticking out and a head leaning against the mama's back whenever you walked past. Men usually have pantsuits made of pagne as well. For important ceremonies, people get matching pagne, which is exactly what we did.

For our stage of nearly 50 people, having our own pagne uniform meant that we had to come to an agreement as to what our pagne pattern would be. To make the process easier, we chose two representatives each from the agriculture stage and the health stage to select and purchase pagne for us a few weeks before our swearing in ceremony. Each volunteer either bought three or six meters depending on what they were looking to make. The representatives returned with a muted pagne pattern, one of white lines with yellow and dark blue borders forming shapes over a dark blue checkered pattern background. I purchased three meters of the fabric to make a button-up collared short sleeve shirt.

About a week before our ceremony, each volunteer was given invitations to the ceremony to give to our host families. Since we could not accommodate all of everyone's families, each volunteer received two invitations to give out. In my case, Martine, Amira, and Rayan had school and my host dad was in Douala. My second invitation went to Yolande, our neighbor who was oftentimes found sitting on the patio with Fortune at the end of the workday.

I was able to pick up my shirt and pants I had made from a different pagne the day before we swore in. I wish that I had more time because the pants were tight, something that was the case with any pair of pants I tried to have made throughout my time in Cameroon. I could barely button them as I tried them on but I didn't have time for any adjustments to be made. The next day, I went to put on my swearing-in clothes and the pant zipper immediately broke. There I was, frantically digging through my bags for a pair of black pants that would work as a replacement. I finally found the one pair of black pants I brought with me to staging, just to find them dirty and wrinkled with no time to clean them. I was stuck. Luckily, however, it was just the pant zipper. I used my pagne shirt to cover it up as best I could.

After walking to the training center and taking a short bus ride we were at our site for swearing in, Petpenoun Resort. The resort is on a lake with a mountain on the other side. The place is absolutely stunning, with beautiful grass and even a golf course. We had our ceremony next to the lake, and both before and after the ceremony everyone could be found taking photos of one another on the dock and lakeside. I became the personal photographer for Fortune and Yolande. For them, these photos were souvenirs of the ceremony. They would be able to show them off to all of their friends in Foumbot, telling them about the great ceremony they were invited to at such a beautiful place, to celebrate their white daughter. Of course, I made the time to also get photos with my fellow stage-mates, with my program managers, and with the Peace Corps flag.

Finally, it was time for the ceremony itself. It was kicked

off by a traditional Bamoun dance, since Foumbot is a part of Bamoun country. Then, as with any graduation ceremony, there were speeches. We heard from the country director and a representative from the United States Embassy. We also heard speeches from two volunteers, one in French and one in Fulfilde, the language of the Adamawa region of Cameroon. At one point, we were called up one by one to the front to be properly introduced, since we weren't going to be walking across a stage as if at a graduation. Finally, we all stood as one in our matching pagne, lifted our right hands, and took the oath of a federal employee. With those few words, we were officially volunteers.

I didn't feel any different than I had the moments before I took my oath. I was definitely ready to head to site, but that wasn't a new feeling. I think part of it was that we spent our last week of training in preparation to move. I had already felt the gratification of passing my presentations and French exam, and had already done all of the paperwork. The ceremony instead was icing on the cake for surviving ten weeks of intense training. I have to admit that my brain was already looking towards all of the packing that I still had to do, the goodbyes I would have to make the following morning, and the unknown that lay ahead of me as soon as the bus would drop me off in Bafoussam, the regional capital of the West region. I understood the ceremony was for the previous ten weeks, but to me it was more like a kickoff to the next 24 months.

Once we took our oath and a group photo, it was time

to eat. Anything called a ceremony in Cameroon must have food with it, and our swearing in ceremony was no exception. There was a wide variety of food and dessert, including the staples of rice, potatoes, and corn fufu. Corn fufu is ground corn mixed with water and beaten into a thick paste while being heated. The balls of paste are usually separated into different banana leave and eaten by hand, dipped in sauce. There was the volunteer favorite of poisson brassé, which is fish grilled over an open flame, and also normally eaten by hand. It is usually served with cassava baton, which is essentially a paste created by cassava tubers that are steamed in banana leaves. I don't like baton, but others absolutely love it and would always get it with their poisson brassé. There were several meat options and tons of fruit. I gorged. While I didn't know what the future held, I knew that I had always been a terrible cook and that living by myself meant that this was likely the best food that I was going to see for some time. Before we knew it, it was time to head back to Foumbot and face the realities of packing and getting ready to leave the next day. But for those few hours we got to celebrate what can sometimes be forgotten as a success — simple survival.

5

I left Fortune and my homestay family having spent two months of training surrounded by both other Americans and Peace Corps staff. As such, I had zero clue what to expect when I was moving to a new village, called Banza, also in the West region. I had never been there and had seen no pictures of my house. I had the trunk I was given when I arrived at my homestay, my suitcase, my hiking backpack, my regular backpack, and an additional giant cloth zippered bag, all filled with what I had packed for two years of service and all that I had accumulated during ten weeks of training. After a bus took the newly sworn in volunteers who would be living in the West region to the regional capital of Bafoussam, we went our separate ways. There I was met an education volunteer then also serving in Banza who helped me get to the bus station while I lugged all of my things. We bought our tickets, my bags and trunk were unceremoniously thrown on top of the bus, and off we went. I had never gone

31

this way out of Bafoussam before and I kept my face was glued to the left side window as we chugged into the hills on the way to Dschang, the capital city of Menoua division. I was told to pay attention because we would in fact be getting off before Dschang, and next time I would have to know when to tell the driver to stop since I'd be traveling by myself.

After getting off, putting my things onto motos and getting onto one myself, we were on the way to my concession. I tried to take everything in as we passed, knowing that this was going to be home for the next two years. It was like arriving at college to move in, understanding that you had no idea what lay in store but knew it was already home. I saw concessions of several mud brick houses scattered between farmland. I later learned that the Bamiléké people are polygamous, and that each concession had a house for the man of the family and separate houses for each wife and her children. I learned that in Banza, instead of having a village center and farms surrounding it, the houses were spread out around the farmland. I tried and failed to keep track of the turns we were taking until we made it to my concession. The gate was closed and we were locked out. Within five minutes my counterpart (the work partner assigned to a volunteer), Noumedem Angilbert, was there but he didn't have the key either. Angilbert is an older man, with nothing longer than a graying stubble on his head and face. In time, I would come to know that he is one of the hardest workers I ever met, not only farming cash crops but also vegetables, tapping palm wine, and raising animals semi-intensively. Oftentimes I went to my farm, which was right next to his, early in the morning, and I would see him shuffling around in his pajamas and slide sandals, feeding his rabbits.

We waited some more for Ndoungni Thomas, the guardian of the concession, to arrive with the keys. Pa Thomas, as he insisted on being called, is a short man who almost every morning can be heard singing as he putzes around the concession, wearing the same t-shirt, pants, and blazer that are all much too big for him with a green and beige beanie on his head. He speaks a rapid fire mixture of French and Yemba (the patois), and my comprehension was not helped by the fact that he is missing all of his top teeth. He lived in our concession, overseeing both the house and the neighboring farmland for my landlord. It took us a while to get used to one another, but he was always making sure I was safe.

Pa Thomas arrived no more than ten minutes later and soon I was looking at the inside of my apartment. It was almost bare, except for a bed frame and mattress in the bedroom, a small cement counter in the tiny kitchen area, and a table with chairs on the patio. It was mine to create a home for myself. I had a great house, especially by Peace Corps standards. Very different from many of the surrounding concessions, it was one cement house with the main living space upstairs and two separate apartments downstairs. The large upstairs had its own doors up the hill from the apartments below. It had been divided into two apartments by sheets of plywood and living on one side was more than enough space for me. I had a large living room, a significantly sized bedroom, a small kitchen, and an inside bathroom.

It also included a wide balcony with a tremendous view out into the valley, a view I loved especially in the early mornings. I would often sit with a mug of tea and my journal while the sun rose over the opposite ridge. It was a great place to sit and relax, especially since it was private. People could not see up from the road onto the patio and call out to me, which given my introvert tendencies was perfect. I hung a hammock out there and many afternoons I could be found there reading. It was also the perfect spot for my clothes and my crops to dry out since it was enclosed. I didn't have to worry about being home as I left things up there, for days (or in the case of my crops, months) at a time out of fear that someone would take them.

It was the toilet, however, that made my house even better. I had spent my homestay using a latrine, and I had gotten used to it. Some people prefer the latrine, but I preferred a toilet whenever possible. I did not have running water. Instead it was a bucket flush toilet, meaning that every time that I went I would have to dump water into it as a flushing mechanism. I learned the art of just how much water to pour in at just the right angle to make sure that things went down instead of up.

Another huge benefit was that I had electricity, at least

most of the time. I could read easily at night whether it be a Kindle or a printed book. I could use my computer to do reports, to watch too many movies and entire television series, and to write entries for my blog. I did learn the importance of making sure that my spare battery packs and my Luci solar light were always fully charged. The power would go out, more often in rainy season, for a few hours up to a few days. It was frustrating, if only because I wanted consistency. I either wanted the electricity to be on full time or I wanted to learn to live without it. This wish for consistency might have jinxed me, as in February 2018 I had no power for nearly the entire month. During an early season rainstorm, a lightning bolt hit a tree that knocked down a power line. I was finally getting the hang of living a dark life with the sun setting early each evening when I was blinded while on the couch one night as the power came back on.

I was also grateful for my tin roof. While most volunteers in Cameroon had solid roofs, that is not the case for volunteers worldwide. For example, I could have had a thatch roof instead. I wouldn't say that my roof was completely solid, however. The main downside was that there was no ceiling beneath the roof. As a result I had numerous leaks, and any time I called the technician to fix them, new ones would appear. I learned to stop calling the technician and to just put some duct tape down on the floor so that I would always know where to keep the bowls to collect falling water. Eventually, I just left containers under the biggest leaks year-round and would clean up the others with a towel once the rain had stopped. While I would have had leaks eventually, a ceiling would have kept them from being as numerous and as intense. The lack of ceiling also meant that there was nothing to absorb the sounds of rain or birds landing. It made drizzles seem like downpours and downpours keep me from hearing myself think. When I was on the phone when those downpours hit, I would have to put headphones in and yell to hear and be heard. Even then oftentimes I would have to give up.

One aspect that ended up being rather critical to my happiness was that I usually had decent phone service. To you, this may make me sound like a phone addict. To me, it meant that I was able to call my support network. I called my dad on WhatsApp almost every day. During rainy season this service wasn't great, but there was a single spot in the backyard that always had it. I had to learn to be still when making WhatsApp calls because if I walked around like I prefer to do when on the phone, I would inevitably lose service. There was a rock next to the fence that I would sit on, which I started calling phone call rock. Other volunteers aren't as lucky. I visited someone who had zero service in her immediate area, and had to walk ten minutes to the local school to get enough service to make a WhatsApp phone call.

My life was made easier by the fact that my house was partially furnished when I arrived. As I mentioned, my landlord, Zogning Francois, who lived full-time in Douala, had left a bed, mattress, table, and chairs. It was great to arrive and already have those since I am terrible about going to buy furniture. I'm someone who slept on an air mattress for three weeks simply because I didn't want to go buy my own bed and mattress when moving to Boston. I could feel the individual bed frame boards through the mattress, but at least I had something off of the ground to sleep on. In my first six months, if I was home I was either in that bed, at the balcony table, or on the floor resting on a prayer mat I had purchased in Dschang. All of my books, clothes, and farm tools were organized in cardboard boxes leftover from care packages.

I eventually realized that I hadn't taken the proper time to make my house a true home and decided to go out to buy my own furniture. I didn't go crazy at the carpenter; instead I bought a plastic set of stacked bins for dishes, a raffia bamboo wood shelving unit, a raffia bamboo wood chair, a desk, and a couch. I moved my trunk to my living room and put pagne over it as a tablecloth, thus creating a coffee table. I hung up a big map of the northern portion of Africa, a map of the world, and a map of the United States. I hung up a ton of photos that would inevitably fall down no matter how many times I taped them back up. I hung up a page from the Cape Cod Times of the Cotuit 4th of July Parade to remind me of home. Little by little, I was making the apartment my own.

While I was the only person to live in my apartment, by no means was I alone. I always had the company of insects, lizards, and mice. Usually I did well on ignoring my small roommates, but it was easier with the insects and lizards than it was with the mice. I didn't mind them until they got into my food. I put out glue traps and poison for them, killing some, including one that I actually had to scrape off the floor with a machete since it got off the cardboard before getting stuck to the floor, but they soon learned to avoid the traps. I once was trying to get a mouse out of my kitchen when it jumped over a glue trap and then climbed up the entire wall and over the other side. They dug passageways through the cement. They even left mousy doos, as my mother called them, in my dishes. I started to guard my food better by putting it in my trunk, in closed plastic bins, and in hanging plastic bags. They crossed the line when they got into my care package food that I had left in my trunk, but there was nothing I could do. I could only protect the remaining food by moving it into the bins and bags. When the food was out of reach, they started to try and explore more in an attempt to find some. No less than five fell into my water buckets and drowned, including two in my family's bucket when they came to visit. Eventually we came to peacefully coexist, even if that meant I was wearing earplugs at night to help me pretend they weren't scurrying around my house.

Making a house a home does not just come from what you do on the inside. To me, it involves becoming a part of the community through integration. Integration is highly emphasized at Pre-Service Training since it helps improve overall happiness by easing loneliness, helps improve personal security since if your neighbors know you they'll look out for you, and helps improve your ability to get work done. I took some time every day for the first few months to hike around, introducing myself to people whenever I could. I explored, finding shortcuts and new paths by streams. Both education volunteers in Banza had clubs at the local bilingual high school where they taught. I would go there each week to not only help but to be seen as a part of the community. I learned some of the greetings in Yemba as a demonstration of my effort to make Banza my home as well.

Another strategy was to go to the market every fourth day. The Bamiléké live on an eight-day weekly calendar. There was a small market day on the fourth day of the week and a large market day on the eighth day. Banza itself did not have a market, but as a smaller village which was part the bigger village of Baleveng, (sort of like a village in a town) everyone would go the three plus miles to the Baleveng market. The Baleveng market ended up being one of my favorite places to go, and I could be frequently found there even when it wasn't market day. While my village was technically Banza, I treated the larger village of Baleveng as my village as well. While still three miles away from home, the Baleveng market was the closest place for me to buy food for the week. Almost every market day I would walk around and say hello to the vendors who I had gotten to know, some of whom I never purchased from in my two years in village, such as the fish man who learned I didn't buy from him because I just didn't know how to cook and the woman who sold blankets. The market area was large relative to most village marketplaces. People would come from cities as far away as Yaoundé and Douala to buy and sell crops and livestock. On the road, people sold giant bags of avocados and big bundles of plantains to travelers passing through. Buses would stop on the side of the road as bag after bag of crops were loaded on top. Cars would have trunks full with the lid open, everything held in place by rubber cords.

The rest of the market was clearly divided based on what was being sold. There were areas for vegetables, tubers, livestock, cooking utensils, blankets, Western clothes, pagne, fish, traditional clothes, and tailors. There was also a small section for the frip, which is where vendors pile clothes onto tarps on the ground for people to rifle through. These clothes, a mixture of already made pagne clothes and Western clothes, were much cheaper than the clothes you can find on hangers in the Western clothing section of the market. There was also a small technology section near the main road where people could buy cell phones and sim cards.

Before making my promenade through the market I could be found at a restaurant run by a trio of women – Nanfack Sidonie, Kentsop Veronique, and Danchi Gisele. After hiking the three miles to get there, I would always eat a spaghetti omelet, a Cameroonian breakfast staple. It is a handful of spaghetti held together with an egg or two mixed together with tomatoes, onions, and other available vegetables. It can even be eaten as a sandwich, with avocado on top. When eating at the restaurant, promenading around the market, and sitting at one of the boutiques, people would chat with me, giving me an opportunity to get to know them, learn more about Baleveng, and improve my French language skills.

Eventually, people started to know who I was. I no longer got strange looks from people as I said hello to everybody, even if I didn't know them. They had heard that the new white girl was friendly. After a while, I knew people's faces and they knew mine, and we would always say hello even though we had no idea what each other's names were. I learned that it wasn't expected of me to say hello to everyone, but it was something that was greatly appreciated. Plus, it allowed me to practice my French. Little by little, I was able to improve my French to the point where I didn't even have to think about it anymore. I didn't have to do translations in my head and instead simply spoke French. I wasn't perfectly fluent, but I was able to achieve all of my work and have broad ranging conversations with minimal issues.

One day about two months into my time in Baleveng, I was stopped by someone I had waved to while passing their concession. He told me his name was Timolean and that he was in village for a week while he prepared his land for the next planting season. He had caught a cane rat on his property that morning and told me that if I came back at 1:00 p.m. I could eat some. Both out of fascination as to what cane rat was like and knowing how rude it would have been to say no to free food, I came back at 1:00 p.m. and ate a rat leg. This only happened because I was making an effort to say hello to people I was passing. If I had simply walked passed his house and not said anything, I would have missed such a typical Peace Corps moment.

Another day near the end of my service, I was at the market

chatting with Tsakue Roni, one of the farmers I worked with. He told me that I was not the first American to ever live in Baleveng, but I was the first to become a part of the village family. I don't think that he knew either of my site-mates, who lived and worked primarily in Banza instead of across a much wider part of the 88 square kilometers of Baleveng like I did. But no matter what any Americans did before me or while I was there, what hit home to me was that he considered me a part of the community and that others around him when he said this to me had agreed. A part of that was the speaking tradition at my alma mater, Washington and Lee University. The tradition is students and staff always saying hi to one another as they pass, even if they are strangers; being a part of the same Washington and Lee community is enough to warrant a friendly hello. I brought the speaking tradition with me to Cameroon. It allowed me to rapidly become a part of the Baleveng community, and for me to consider Baleveng to be home.

6

Just one week after leaving my homestay, I was already back for Fortune and my host dad's wedding. It was my first Cameroonian ceremony, and it was one that I will always remember. The entire day highlighted many parts of Cameroonian culture that I had seen during my training. This included the huge volume of food that gets eaten at ceremonies, how late everything starts (a lesson I would learn all too well throughout my service), how little people sleep the weekend of a party, and the social acceptability of sleeping in public for those looking to catch a quick nap. It was a lot to take in for the 21 hours that I was back in Foumbot.

When I arrived on Saturday morning at around 9:00 a.m., I had no idea where I was supposed to be or what I was supposed to be doing. All I knew was that Fortune had asked me to come as early in the day as possible, but she was nowhere to be found. I also couldn't find my wedding uniform, which she had taken back to the tailor for me. Similar to my swearing-in pants, the tailor sewed my pagne too tight, to the point that I couldn't even get it over my head the first time I tried it on. Unlike in the situation with my swearing-in pants, I had time to get it taken out but Martine had to pick it up for me since I wasn't in Foumbot anymore.

When I arrived, the concession was already mobbed with people. While seeing a concession lined with plastic chairs and tons of people milling about became a regular sight at future ceremonies, it was a new one for me at the time. Everyone, mostly women, were dressed nicely in various pagne patterns. They seemed to stop and stare at me as I walked in, the white girl wearing khakis and a t-shirt, both covered in dust from traveling in the dry season. I asked someone at the door where I could find Martine because I did not recognize a single person out of all the people in the concession. She had looked out for me during my homestay and I figured Fortune was busy getting ready. But Martine was not there. She and the family were on their way back from the traditional ceremony the day before in Fortune's home village. Instead of sitting around with strangers, I went to where I knew I could find a familiar face — Yolande's house, the neighbor who had come to my swearing-in ceremony just a week prior. Throughout the day, I ate two big bowls of corn fufu as I relaxed in the relative peace of her house waiting for things to start.

The civil ceremony was the first of two ceremonies for the day, and it was supposed to start at 2:00 p.m. at the town hall.

About an hour before it was supposed to start, I was able to get Martine on the phone and she directed me to where my dress was stashed. I put it on right away thinking that we should be leaving at any moment to make it to the ceremony on time. Yolande and I didn't end up leaving until after 2:00 p.m. She had to convince me that arriving at 2:00 p.m. would be too early. As it was we were still too early; the ceremony didn't start until 4:00 p.m.

For well over an hour, everyone stood around in their wedding pagne, having changed since I saw them in the morning, waiting for the ceremony to start. Then the car with the family showed up. You would have thought that a team had just come back from winning the state championships. There was a small band playing, people were blowing whistles, and people surrounded the car to dance. The civil ceremony itself was standing room only. I ended up watching through an open window in the back because I had no idea that there would not be enough space. I could see well enough and, given my relatively low French level at the time, I wouldn't have understood much of what was going on even if I was in the front row.

The family left the civil ceremony and got back into the car to the same fanfare. Then everyone jumped onto motos and squished into cars. I thought we were going back to the concession for a quick break before the reception which was supposed to start at 8:00 p.m. I thought wrong. We ended up zooming through town, honking and yelling and creating a giant scene to celebrate the newlyweds. Some people even stood up as the motos they were on flew along the main road.

I had learned from the civil ceremony that there was no way the reception was going to actually start at 8:00 p.m, so after another meal — this time of rice and fish — I made sure to take a nap on Yolande's couch before heading over. I had learned that the reception was not going to end until 6:00 a.m. and I needed to rest up as much as possible.

Getting into the reception itself made me feel like I was a VIP at a club. I was given a car ride from Fortune's concession to the party hall. When I arrived, there was a line of people at the gate, all holding invitations that served as our tickets. Fortune's brother saw me and brought me straight to the front of the line. I squeezed through a small opening in the gate and was immediately brought to my table with other members of the extended family. The room was packed with giant round tables that could seat over ten people. Once everyone was seated, it was nearly impossible to move my chair in any direction, and I was essentially stuck.

The reception itself didn't start until after midnight and it did indeed last until 6:00 a.m. After speeches and a buffet dinner, there were plenty of performances. There were family members, either amazing cover artists or actual famous artists based on the reactions to introductions, and traditional Bamoun performers. It is difficult to describe the blur that was those first three hours other than by saying that the performances were incredible and I know I will never see a string of performances like that again.

At around 3:00 a.m., the newly married couple stood up and started calling specific people to the main aisle that also served as a small dance floor. I was honored to be one of the 16 people asked to come up, even though I had no idea what it was for. After maneuvering my way through the maze of chairs and tables, I quickly learned that each person was matched with a dance partner, since the men and women were clearly placed on opposite sides of the aisle. We all danced to the same song, with my partner twirling me around gently. I was touched that they wanted to include me in this. After the song finished I got confused that we were told to stay in place. They then asked a person who had made a speech earlier a question, but I didn't catch a word of his answer. Immediately after, Fortune was telling me I won! It turns out that I had been asked to enter a dance contest. Different important members of the crowd were asked to select who won in their eyes. I don't think knowing it was a competition would have made me dance any differently but I found it amusing that my partner and I won when I had absolutely no idea what was going on.

The dance contest was followed by the gift giving portion of the evening. Unlike in the United States where you can order online and ship the gift straight to their home, people at this wedding brought all of the gifts to the reception. This still confuses me, since most of the people were at the concession earlier in the day and it would have saved the newlyweds a lot of effort if the gifts had been left at the house. Everyone got in line with their gift in hand and one by one handed it to the bride and groom. I realized that since I had no idea what a Cameroonian wedding entailed, I didn't think to bring the gift with me to the reception. I had left my gift at Yolande's house when we left, thinking I was saving Fortune some effort.

The gift giving ended and the dancing began at 4:30 a.m. At that point I was exhausted, both physically from being up for about 23 hours at that point, and mentally from dealing with the crowds and many people wanting to talk to or *derange* (French for harass) the white girl. I did try dancing a little bit but whenever I tried, people would try to hold me closely while dancing, which was something I was not comfortable with. I chose to leave the dance aisle and sat down at one of the tables. I noticed that there were people sleeping around the room and decided to follow suit and put my own head down on the table. I didn't actually fall asleep, but it was a nice excuse to finally have some privacy. I made sure to rejoin the party after a bit of mental reprieve and we finally hopped back on motos to head back to the concession a few hours later.

It was a wild and incredible 21 hours, and an experience for which I will forever be thankful to Fortune, for making sure that I was invited. I was taking up a seat and I was another mouth to feed, but I was her American daughter and she made sure I was there and that I participated. If it wasn't for Fortune's insistence, I would have never experienced this type of celebration and there would have been a gap in my cultural education of Cameroon.

7

I had the good fortune of being welcomed at many traditional ceremonies across Baleveng. People understood my desire to learn more about the Bamiléké culture, and they were willing to share that with me. I was able to attend many funerals, a ceremony celebrating twins, and a traditional house warming ceremony. There are other ceremonies that are private and just for the family. While I was unable to attend those, my community made sure to educate me on their practices.

The Funerals

The most common ceremony by far was the traditional funeral. There are funerals almost every single weekend of the year. I was confused at first given the size of Baleveng, wondering, "how are there any people left if we keep celebrating funerals?" I eventually learned that people are buried alongside their ancestors, no matter where they die.

When people pass away they are brought home from even as far away as the United States to make sure they are buried properly.

Funeral ceremonies, called deuils (pronounced "doys"), are nothing like they are in the United States. Instead of being held in churches or at funeral homes and generally being events of sadness, funerals there are celebrations of life. Music is blasted from Friday afternoon until Sunday morning, which is how I got my first taste of funerals. Even though in the beginning I never knew who was being celebrated or even most people attending the funerals, I could hear the music as it echoed through the valley that my balcony overlooked. Sleep was difficult when there was a funeral in my immediate area, and was impossible on the two occasions when they were at houses right next to mine. I'd find myself hoping that the power would go out so I could finally hear myself think. That moment when the music would stop was always such a relief. It was bizarre to immediately feel more tired because you were no longer completely focused on blocking out the noise. It also made me appreciate the normal peacefulness of Banza after not having quiet while these celebrations went on.

People would come in from all over Cameroon, and even from outside Cameroon, to celebrate at funerals. Even late into the second year of my service, I would become the new white girl again on those weekends and these visitors would inevitably be surprised to learn that I actually lived there. These visitors would fight for places to sleep, and many times the apartment on the other side of my house was essentially rented out for the weekend to those willing to pay for a bed or a spot on the floor. Others would simply sleep in public and in the morning try to find a private place to bathe. One time I gave up on my sleep and went to open my windows to let some fresh air in, just to be surprised by a naked woman squatting underneath the windows cleaning herself, staring up at me as if accusing me of having the audacity to interrupt her bath. While the idea of leaving to go to a quiet hotel in Dschang did cross my mind whenever I heard that a funeral would be in our area, I knew that it would be disrespectful. Especially when the funerals were at the houses next to mine, I was expected to show up to at least part of it, and given how welcoming my neighbors were, it would have been a slap in the face to leave town.

The first funeral I attended was about a month into my service. I was privileged to meet Tsongnang Guemegni Gaston, the King of Baleveng and someone who I would end up doing some of my work with. He is a hardworking king who wants only the best for his village, and has hopes for modernization after traveling to several cities in the United States and parts of Europe. He oftentimes would be sporting the University of Texas shirt he got on his trip to the United States. He also knows the importance of tradition, and wanted to make sure that as someone who would be spending the next two years in his village, I learn that aspect of life there. In our first meeting, he invited me to attend a funeral with him that following weekend. As someone who was eager to learn about my new home culture, I jumped at the opportunity.

Just a few days later I found myself surrounded by princes in the King's living room. I felt out of place, as if I shouldn't be there, both as a woman and as an American. I had no idea what was going on or where the funeral was going to be, and the princes were all speaking Yemba when I could still only speak passable French. But the King wanted me there. We soon hopped into cars along with some of their wives and headed down dusty roads into the hills of Baleveng. Our arrival was something that I hope to never forget. There was a giant crowd of people when we arrived, all working to catch a glimpse of His Majesty as we walked into the concession. One person had the responsibility of holding a giant umbrella over the King's head everywhere he went. Some people were blowing whistles while others were shooting shotguns into the air. Our group was led to a special tent, with the men sitting in front and the women sitting behind. We kept standing as the King took a lap around the concession dancing and we stayed that way until he sat down. Every time he stood up we were expected to stand and stay standing until he returned to his chair. Our tent was filled with water, sodas, and alcohol for the King and his group to drink while enjoying the ceremony, and once it was over we were led to a house to have a meal. I quickly learned that food and drink were as huge a part of ceremonies as the music. The women put extra food in their bags to bring to the children they left at home, a trick I used later to bring extra food back for Pa Thomas.

I have to admit that I do not remember much else about that first funeral, especially since we ended up going to a second one immediately after. I think part of it is that I attended so many ceremonies, including more with the King and others on my own, that they have blended together. No funeral was exactly the same, but they all held similar traditional aspects. Close friends and family wore a matching pagne uniform. Family members also wore a traditional Bamiléké vest — blue with white lines forming shapes and frayed at the waist — while carrying a handle with horse hair attached that was waved around as they danced. There were usually traditional dancers who wore brown beaded instruments on their calves, creating noise with every movement as they danced to the beat of traditional drums. There is one particular performance where a group of people, all wearing big tan square masks with black material surrounding the head and eye-holes surrounded by red, walk into the concession in a line, but spaced wide apart, purposefully taking a step only every thirty seconds as they make a big circle around the concession before making their way back out. They look around during each step as if the eyes of the masks were staring into the crowd. At some point, either before or after those dancers but never during their performance, people related to the deceased go into the center of the concession and form a big dancing circle that moves to the beat of fast paced drumming. Many of the family members hold big framed photos of the deceased as they dance around the circle. These ceremonies usually last around an hour or two before everyone disperses to different neighboring concessions for food and drink while the music continues.

After going to a few funerals, I started seeing some that were actually very different from others that I had been to. These ones had a casket in the middle of the concession and a priest while the others did not. I had no idea that they were two completely difference ceremonies because everyone uses the same name for them for both of them. They were actually the burial and the celebration. The burial almost always had a casket, a priest, a public cry, and speeches from the family members. This was a sadder event, and more similar to funerals in the United States. The end of it was always marked by the family members, all dressed in the same uniform pagne, carrying the casket from the center of the concession to where the other family members had been buried. I once went to a burial for a person important enough that they held it in a large church and there were tents outside for hundreds of extra seats. The traditional celebration is the true deuil, and it celebrates the spirit. There are no Christian elements to the deuil since it is purely a ceremony from the traditional religion. This can be held anytime from the same weekend to five years after the burial, depending mostly on the costs and the ability of the family to host the ceremony.

There is another ceremony related to death, but this is reserved for just the family. Ten years after the initial burial, the body is dug back up and the skull is removed. The rest of the body is put back into the grave while the skull is placed on a mantle next to the skulls of other family members. Sacrifices are regularly made to the ancestors by putting salt, oil, or drink next to the skulls. One of Angilbert's neighbors has so many deceased family members to honor that they were building a mud hut to give them their own small house when I was leaving.

The Twin Ceremony

In the Bamiléké tradition, having twins is considered to be good luck. There are even specific words in Yemba for the parents of twins: *tani* for the father of twins and *mani* for the mother. It is important to have a ceremony to reaffirm the luck that has been given to the family. Bad luck can — and it is believed eventually will — fall on the family if the ceremony is not performed. But, the belief is that bad luck can be reversed later in the twins' lives once the ceremony is performed.

Angilbert is a tani. When his twins were born, he did not throw a proper ceremony for them because he did not have enough money. His twin daughters, in their early 20s, were trying and failing to get visas to study in Italy. He and his first wife Charlotte realized that it must be because they never threw the twin ceremony. To resolve the issue, they threw one in 2019. The most important part of hosting the ceremony is to have food for everyone who stops by. The idea is that they as parents of twins have received a blessing, and they should share that blessing with others through food.

Once everyone else had been fed, the ceremony began. It started with a grand entrance of all of the parents of twins in the village, many of them carrying either a large marmite (a metal pot common in Cameroon) of food or a case of drinks on their heads while the rest rang traditional bells. I was surprised at how many people in the village had given birth to twins. They proceeded to march in a big circle for a few rounds before turning into a small area set up for them to eat together while everyone else patiently waited. Once they finished eating, they exited, marching and dancing in another big circle at the center of the concession. Gone were the food and drink on top of people's heads. Instead, there was a white sheet over the family of the twins as they danced around ringing the traditional bells. After a little bit, the white sheet was removed, and everyone was invited into the circle to dance for awhile and that was it. The twin ceremony is simple but expensive since the parents need to provide enough food for everyone to eat.

The Housewarming Ceremony

Similar in nature to the twin ceremony is the housewarming ceremony. My neighbor built a new house in his concession and invited me to the ceremony which is meant to bring good luck to the house. It was a simple ceremony. It started with the blessing of the house, which was done by the priest. Then someone climbed up a ladder to pour wine onto the house as a sacrifice and to stick a peace tree branch into the gutter to protect the house from evil spirits. Everyone went inside to eat, and it is imperative that everyone is given at least something small. Children snuck in and took a ton of food before the adults were fed. What was left was distributed as best as possible even if it meant that some people were served only a few plantain chips. When leaving, all guests were given a bag of salt and a few chicken flavored cooking cubes. We were meant to give these to our ancestors by leaving them by their skulls in our houses. Clearly, I didn't have any familial skulls in my house, but it would have brought bad luck to both myself and to my neighbor's house should I have refused to take it.

The traditional ceremonies that I was able to witness were heavily focused on people's ancestors and their roots. Based on what I saw and what I learned, it seems that the Bamiléké people regard their ancestors as overseers. They believe that in death, our ancestors are still looking out for us, which is why we must continue to honor them by gifting food and drink to their skulls. We must continue to treat others well, for example through providing food at ceremonies like the twin ceremony and the house warming ceremony, in order for the ancestors of others to look out for us as well. This was important even for those who practiced Christianity. It seemed as if they couldn't risk the repercussions of mistreating their ancestors and those of others. Even those who followed the teachings of the Bible and attended church every Sunday still both partook in and put on these ceremonies.

Ceremonies were a fascinating aspect to my experience in Cameroon, especially as someone who studied religion at Washington & Lee University. I was part of a community that mixed religions, and did it in such an open way. It was refreshing to see the way that they made their beliefs work for them, and that they were able to successfully do this, seemingly without conflict. I was among people who saw the value of traditions and held onto them, even if they no longer fully believed in the reasons for them. I think there are some things that we all can learn from the Bamiléké in this regard, most glaringly acceptance, flexibility, and the importance of not forgetting your past.

8

It is impossible for any Peace Corps Cameroon volunteer to survive without buckets. While I understood the necessity of them conceptually before leaving the United States, nothing could prepare me for the actuality of what bucket life was like. It was completely different to be personally dependent on what are essentially giant plastic cups with handles for over two years. During my service I needed buckets for just about every part of daily life, from collecting water outside and catching rain water inside to bathing, washing clothes and dishes, and flushing the toilet.

This was especially important during my first few months at site. My ten weeks of training were at the end of the rainy season, and when I finally arrived to my new home it was officially dry season. I had no idea if the well that supplied the outdoor spigot in my concession would run dry or if I could rely on it for my collection of tens of gallons of water almost each and every day. As the dry season continued, I learned that I could not, and that I would have to start guarding my water. About six weeks into dry season, the spigot stopped working in the middle of the day. I would open the spigot but the only thing that would come out was a gurgling sound as if there was some water at the bottom of the pipe but not enough for any to pour into my bucket. I was told that when this happened, all of the water collected in the well was gone and that we had to wait for it to "recharge." I realized that I had to compete with my neighbors to be able to get water, since one well supplied several spigots and there simply was not enough for everyone. I had to get to the spigot in the morning before they used up all of the water that collected in the well overnight. I felt guilty about that competition, knowing that whatever water I was taking could have been going to a neighbor, especially considering that if I didn't live in my apartment, nobody else would. But there was nothing I could do about that guilt except not waste any of the water that I did collect.

One advantage I had was that my landlord Francois had left a big blue barrel that had been used to store chemicals in a previous life. It was washed out and we used it to store extra water in the event that we needed it. I could choose to not compete for the water in the spigot and instead use the barrel. But I had no idea when the spigot would stop working permanently and I knew that the barrel of water would not last forever. I was good at conserving water, but I wasn't the only one who had access to the barrel. Pa Thomas was using it as well. Since he lived in the concession, he had the same water issues that I did, and also used the blue barrel when the spigot wasn't working in the afternoons. However, he wouldn't refill it when the water was flowing again. Whenever there was the need and opportunity I took the time to refill the blue barrel. I wondered if and when the spigot would not turn back on and wanted to be as prepared as possible in the event it did happen.

I think it was the best strategy I could have come up with. I can't tell whether or not it worked well because the water ran out at the same time as a big funeral in village. During the first weekend in February, Francois came back to village with numerous guests who stayed in the apartment on the other side of the house. These guests needed to use water to flush the toilet and to bathe, and given the number of guests that we had it was a lot of water. Instead of using the spigot, they immediately used the blue barrel. I didn't worry about it because it had happened before, and each time I would refill the blue barrel once they left. But once the guests left on Sunday morning, I went to fill up my buckets to find a very weak stream of water filling it up. Before even a quarter of one bucket had been filled, the water stopped. When I went to use the blue barrel, I found that it wasn't even halfway filled with water. The spigot never turned back on that February. I tried to open it every day when I left the house and every day when I returned home. All I got for the entire month of February was the gurgling noise which indicated that there wasn't any water available.

To get any water that February I had to walk nearly a

quarter of a mile down a steep incline to a little stream. Neighbors warned me that the water from the steam was not potable, and they strongly recommended against using it for drinking, cooking, or for even washing my dishes. I was able to use it to flush my toilet and clean my clothes, but I wasn't strong enough to make several trips to carry tens of gallons up the steep hill every day. I ended up taking water conservation to the extreme. For basically a month I ate only packets of beef jerky that my dad sent to me in care packages and hard boiled eggs. The idea was that I could reuse the same water to boil the eggs every day and I didn't have to "waste" the water to clean it out between meals. It shouldn't be a surprise that I ended up losing a lot of weight at this point, and it took me a long time to gain it back. I stopped taking bucket baths, opting to use wet wipes to take dry showers instead. I would use as little water as possible to flush, and even then I only flushed when I pooped. I prayed that I wouldn't get a bout of diarrhea, not from a health or discomfort standpoint but from the perspective that I would have to use too much water flushing if that were to happen and if I was sick I wouldn't have the energy to hike down into the valley to get more.

But throughout that I learned how to be better prepared for dry season. When it came around a second time around a year later I was all set. 12 months into my service I had three buckets, two large basins, and two water jugs. I kept the large basins filled with water and refused to use them unless it was an emergency, like a dreaded case of diarrhea. When I had site visitors for a week, if they used the water from the basin I would make them refill it almost immediately. I felt a bit badly but at the same time I refused to be left without as much water stored as possible, and those volunteers needed to learn the bucket life as well. As with the year before, I almost religiously refilled the blue barrel. I kept every plastic water bottle over the year and filled them up to store over 20 extra gallons of water devoted for cooking and drinking. Of course, after all of the preparation the water in the well never again dried out for any significant length of time. But at least I slept a little better knowing that I was ready for the worst, even if I was almost constantly worried that I would be forced to again take the extreme measures that I took in 2018. I still can't eat beef jerky and I'm not sure that I'll ever be able to eat it again without flashing back to that month.

What I don't think people ever truly understood when I said that I lived out of buckets was that I had to use buckets for basically everything. The three major ones were bathing, washing clothes, and washing dishes. I would dream of the day that I would return to the western world if only to throw clothing or dishes and soap into some sort of machine and press start. For each of these you have to go through the effort of collecting water. I was lucky to have the spigot. I never had to use a true well, the one with a bucket attached to a rope and a pulley.

Collecting the water was just step one in a long process, such as the process of washing my clothes. At home I used to get annoyed with people who complained about having to wash their laundry or saying that they didn't have the time to do it. Washing laundry in the United States is mostly sitting around waiting for the machines that do the actual work. You can throw the laundry in the washing machine late the night before you need the clothes, and then wake up early and throw it in the drier. I'm not sure if I will ever be able to keep my mouth shut when I hear these complaints and while a part of that is my sense of timeliness, it mostly comes from the fact that for over two years of my life I didn't have the option.

Instead of being able to throw my clothes in the machine the night before, I had to perfectly time when I did my laundry. I would have to do it in the morning to give my clothes a chance of drying by the end of the day. If they were still damp, I would have to leave them hanging outside overnight. I detested that because I didn't know what bugs would make homes out of the clothes that I chose to wash. Additionally, instead of washing clothes the night before I needed them, I had to wash my clothes a full three days earlier. There was no washing clothes the night before you needed them because there was the chance of tumbo flies if even by some miracle the clothes managed to dry overnight. Tumbo flies are bugs that lay eggs in your damp clothes after you wash them. To prevent the larvae from burrowing into your skin, you need to let your clothes sit for three days, or kill them by ironing your clothes. During those three days the larvae die. I couldn't wash my clothes on a rainy day since there was no chance that they would dry in time. If I woke up hearing the drizzle on my tin roof, I knew that my laundry plans were scrapped. I would have to wait until my next free sunny morning to try and do my laundry. The sun would shine onto my balcony only in the mornings and if I didn't get my clothes on the line in time, the rainy season humidity (sometimes as high as 95% even if it was sunny) could keep them damp all day no matter how hot it was.

There was also limited space and clothespins to dry out my clothes. When doing laundry, I had to rank my clothes in order of importance, knowing that there was no way that I could actually wash them all. Not only would that have taken way too much time, I simply didn't have the space. I had an extra line that was hung hidden inside of the patio for underwear and bras but that didn't solve the problem. If I chose to wash all of my smaller items like socks and the aforementioned underwear and bras, I would end up running out of clothespins. One time I did that where I used up all of my clothespins just by washing underwear. Needless to say, I was hoping that the sun would dry them quickly to keep anyone taking the path next to our concession from seeing my underwear waving in the breeze.

As a result, laundry was almost always on the "To Do" list. It was never finished in one turn and I refused to spend more than one morning per week doing it, as mornings have and always will be when I am most productive. For almost the entirety of my service, there was a laundry bag half filled with dirty clothes sitting by the bathroom door, begging to be washed.

Finally, no matter how many times I washed the clothes

and no matter how hard I scrubbed, my clothes would never be completely clean. I tried several methods to figure out the best way to get my clothes the cleanest and to be honest I never figured it out. I eventually realized I had to lower my standards for what defined clean clothes. Essentially, they just needed to look clean, even if they weren't. One time through the buckets got rid of any lingering odors from farm work or hiking to the market. What was more important was the visual appearance of the clothes. If I had to choose between pants that I had worn once but had some mud on the scuffs and pants that looked perfectly clean but I had worn five times already since the last time I washed them, I would choose the unwashed pants. Why? Because when people commented on the cleanliness of my clothes, it had to do with any dirt or smudges and no other factor. At home, people aren't forced to make that type of decision unless they managed to forget to throw the clothes in the washing machine the night before. For me, there were many instances where I simply didn't have the time to sit there and scrub at clothes. I did end up choosing a time saving method where I would prioritize washing the clean but used pants by soaking them in soapy water overnight. They didn't need any serious scrubbing, and I didn't need to take the time to make sure I didn't miss any spots. I could give a quick scrub and a dunk into another bucket of clean water before hanging them up to dry and wear three days later. This method worked great for dry fit clothing as well, even if there was mud caked on it, leading me to wear my dry fit clothes much more frequently than any other clothes I brought with me.

Washing clothes was not the only thing I used buckets for. I also used buckets to wash myself. It took a fair bit of physical effort for what is the most relaxing part of my day when I'm in the United States. To put it simply, it involved a ton of squatting. I had to squat to dunk my head directly into the bucket to wash my hair, and hold the squat throughout the shampooing process. I would take a break as I put my hair in a TurbieTwist and put my glasses back on but it was back into the squat for the rest of the bath. I could have bathed standing up by flipping the bucket over my head but that would have been a huge waste of water, and also likely would not have washed me very well. Instead, I stayed squatting next to the bucket as I washed different parts of my body, using as little water as possible while trying to get the soap off. No matter how many different variations of bucket bathing I tried, I was never able to completely get the soap off. By the time I got to a real shower, I would have layers of soap, dirt, and sunscreen caked onto my body. After weeks spend bucket bathing in village, few things felt as good as the hot water of the shower in a hotel or at the Yaoundé transit house. In the moment, they felt life-changing.

Finally, there was the dish washing. I had lived without a dishwasher before, so it was nothing new. But back then, I still had the water pressure to help wash things off, such as leftover cheese sauce from the boxed mac and cheese my dad would send me in care packages. When washing dishes in buckets, you need to make sure to wash the cleanest things first to keep the remaining water as clean as possible for the following dishes. I also should have been washing the dishes every night to free the bucket for other things, but at times that bucket would sit there with more and more dishes in it for days. I sometimes would re-use the same pot to make rice in again, as well as the same serving spoon, bowl and fork, to decrease how often I did dishes.

I think I didn't want to do dishes because I had to squat or sit in a low stool hunched over a bucket to wash them. I did not have a waist-high sink. While that seems straightforward, it is something that people don't think about until they have seen it or heard about it. When my dad and sister came to visit me in January 2019, they had no idea that they had to scrunch themselves over the basin on a tiny stool to wash the dishes after each meal. I was more than happy to let my dad volunteer to do all of the dishes for us. He realized after one time that it was truly a pain in the butt but said that he could put up with it for the week since at least after the week he would never have to do it like that again. Knowing that I will almost certainly never have to wash dishes like that again makes me not take the sink for granted anymore, since even if the water isn't running it is a much more comfortable position from which to wash dishes.

While I often complained about my lack of plumbing, it was not too big of a deal. It just meant more effort to get things done. There was one time, however, that the lack of proper plumbing still haunts me. The toilet started backing up, causing the toilet to not flush well and for a disgusting leak to spring in the bend of the pipe right under my bedroom window.

What had happened was that the PVC piping leading to a giant underground hole was blocked somewhere, which isn't surprising since nothing has been done to it since the house was built 30 years ago. We — and by that I mean Pa Thomas while I watched — ended up having to take off the corner of the pipe that had been leaking to work on unblocking whatever was keeping things from flushing. It started with the toilet and the short pipe that ran underneath my bedroom. I had flush bucket after bucket of water to make sure everything went down. But, since we had taken the corner pipe off, all of that was instead flowing directly to the ground outside of my window. It was more than disgusting, but we were doing what had to be done. Then, Pa Thomas stuck a ten-foot long piece of raffia bamboo wood down it to try to force the blockage down to the hole. We were essentially starting at the top and working our way down to find where the blockage was.

After we were confident that the blockage was not in that first section of underground piping, Pa Thomas broke open the hollow cement block that served as another corner of piping. He put his rain boots on, stepped in the hole, and with his bare hands pulled out grass that had been growing in there and things people had flushed down, including sewage and toothbrushes. He then pushed the stick through the section of underground piping that led directly to a giant hole that served as our septic tank. He finally was able to push the blockage into the hole and when he did, everything that was backed up behind it, including everything still stuck in the first underground pipe, came rushing down. It came down with so much velocity that when it flushed into the hollow cement block where Pa Thomas was standing, it came up like a wave hitting a seawall. From my vantage point on the raised patio it looked like a poop geyser. When everything was put back into place, my job was to take buckets of water and throw them on the ground to force the sewage towards the gutter at the wall opposing the house. All Pa Thomas wanted for his effort was a hot cup of condensed milk in water and a beer, which I was more than happy to provide him given what he had just done for me.

Overall, living out of buckets was a humbling experience. People there do it without a problem because they do not have a choice. By virtue of where I was raised, I became dependent on water technology and I took it for granted. I don't recall a time when we didn't have running water. There have been times when it was a weird color and there have been times that we got alerts to boil it but running water is almost constant. I don't have to worry about a crazy clogged pipe or if I'll have enough water to last the dry season. I just have to turn a handle to flush or to start a shower.

At one point in my service, my brother was redoing his kitchen, and he said that he didn't know what to do while he and his family were struggling without their dishwasher. He was kidding, but the same concept is true for people all over the western world. Unless you have spent time living in a place where those amenities do not exist, you do not have the solutions in your head. The easy solution is what used to be done before the technology became available but for many people, that was generations ago. Thanks to my time in Cameroon, I have the solution. If a sink, shower, dishwasher, or washing machine ever breaks down or becomes unusable, I'm just going to buy some buckets. I can fill them up at a faucet that does work or even at a neighbor's house, or I can do what many people in the world still do and fetch water from the nearest available source.

9

The West region of Cameroon has two seasons — a rainy season that runs from mid-March until mid-November and a dry season from mid-November until mid-March. Throughout my service, I always found myself wishing for the other season. When I first arrived in Baleveng in December 2017, the dry season was already in full swing, having arrived a few weeks early that year. I couldn't wait for rainy season to come back almost immediately, and that was even before my water stopped running in February. But when rainy season finally came around, I was wishing for dry season again. Each season had its advantages and disadvantages. But if I had to choose which one I preferred more, I would have to go with the rainy season. I wished more for the rainy season during the dry season than the other way around, even though rainy season was three times as long.

Dry Season

The dry season was marked by a dry heat that got hotter as the season went on. It would be chilly in the shade if there was a good breeze flowing, but even the breeze wasn't able to help on the hikes to the market if I left any later than 9:00 a.m. The shade was nonexistent after that, and the heat would climb into the mid-80s pretty quickly after the day started in what I considered a chilly low 60s. When I told my dad that it was cold on my 7:00 a.m. hike to the market one morning and told him the temperature, he informed me that I had officially become a weather wimp and that I was going to have a very hard time adjusting to the climate when I came home to Massachusetts in November 2019. He was right. But that didn't stop the fact that the sun would beat down on me as I would try to make the final climb to the market.

The dry heat made farming impossible. That means that for months farmers had no income and no work. They had to guard the food that they grew during the most recent rainy season while they let their land rest. Instead of green crops along the side of the road, there were weeds turned brown from the kicked up dust. Only those who were lucky enough to have plots next to the tiny stream in the valley were able to farm, and even they had to water their plants by buckets, a laborious task. Many of the people in Banza actually had apartments or houses in the bigger cities of Yaoundé and Douala and spent the dry season there.

My first dry season was a very difficult time for me. As I mentioned previously, the water running dry caused me to take drastic measures when it came to my diet and my health. I also didn't have electricity for a month because of an early season rainstorm. There was no ConEd to come out that day or that weekend. The solar charger that I had purchased, which was supposed to be strong enough to charge my computer, didn't work. Even though I was able to leave it out in the sun all day every day, I could only use it to charge my phone twice before it died. I was also sick from the dust. I was hiking daily trying to meet people and thus breathing in enough dust to cause a month long sore throat. There was just no way to get rid of it and my lack of drinking water at the time didn't help matters.

For all of the difficulties of dry season, there is one distinct advantage. During dry season the roads are amazing. I could hike or take a moto whenever I wanted, with no worries as to what time I was leaving (at least from a quality of roads perspective), if it was going to rain during the three-mile hike, or if there would be motos available to take me home. I used that to my advantage, especially in my first dry season. As I mentioned previously, in an effort to try to meet new people I would take a daily hike around the village. The routine of a hike a day helped me immensely. But while I didn't have to time it due to the rain, I did have to time it due to the heat. It was best if I made these hikes earlier in the morning because the sun would beat down for the entire day. I would sometimes hike the mile up to one of the schools to help one of my site-mates with her club group on Wednesday afternoons. I sometimes didn't go simply because it was too hot out. It was not a bad hike, in fact it was mostly flat until an uphill at the end, but the midday sun made it simply exhausting.

The sun was not the only problem — there was the dust. The soil in Baleveng is mostly composed of clay. When that dried up, the dust would get kicked up by cars, motos, and the wind. It would get into your eyes, into your throat, and even onto your teeth. I was constantly covered in dust, and my house was as well. No matter if I kept my hiking shoes at the door and no matter how many times I swept, my floor was always caked in dust. Part of it was because my doors didn't entirely touch the ground, giving an opening for the wind to carry it in. There was also a gap in my roof between the peak and the two sides. The lack of ceiling in my house allowed dust to spread from there. While I swept regularly, I quickly gave up on ever having a completely clean house. For the entirety of my service I had shoes on my feet no matter where I was. To avoid bringing in any extra dust or mud myself, I had my hiking shoes, my house flip flops, and a separate pair of outdoor slide sandals for when I would go search for phone service or collect water.

Rainy Season

Rainy season was much easier for me to survive. I had access to water for cooking, drinking, and cleaning and my crops were able to grow. People in my area were able to work on their farms and some people did come back, if only to plant their corn, beans, and peanuts before heading to the city again. But despite all of its advantages, it had its own slew of problems.

I actually realized the first of the rainy season problems in the middle of the dry season. We had a random thunderstorm pass through during the night. I will never forget it. I woke up at 1:00 a.m. to a constant loud drumming on my roof. At first I was confused because I had spent two months without ever hearing the noise. I quickly realized it was the rain pouring onto my tin roof. It sounded like my roof was about to cave in, and that feeling returned almost every time that it poured down rain. During that first rainstorm, I decided to go out on my balcony to check it out. That was when I realized that I had a big problem with the rain already: leaks. I had leaks in almost every room of my apartment, over five leaks in my living room alone. All of these leaks seemed to coincide with where there was the aforementioned gap in the roof, and no matter how many times I explained that to my landlord and to the technician who would come to my house to plug up any holes, nobody seemed to understand. The technician did fix the other holes but since new ones would pop up every time he came, I gave up and learned to keep bowls in various spots on the floor.

The first time that it rained during the day while I was at site, near the end of February 2017, I was ecstatic. This was after not having water for weeks. I quickly dressed in athletic shorts and a t-shirt and ran outside to enjoy it while it lasted. I had no idea how long the rain was going to last since it wasn't actually rainy season yet. My house had gutters on each side, and each side had a spot from which the water poured off. It was great for collecting water throughout the rainy season because Pa Thomas put the big blue barrel underneath one of them and we collected tens of gallons of water nearly every time it rained. During the course of the first rainstorm, I used one the pour offs to take a fully-clothed shower. The water was absolutely freezing and my clothes got soaked, but I was giddy, and more importantly, my hair was about as clean as it ever got in village. The water rinsed out months' worth of dust and soap scum that had collected in my hair.

The leaks were not the only problems in the rainy season. From a work perspective, rains could make giving trainings very challenging, since whenever it rained nobody would show up. I could hike for three miles in the rain and mud and not a single person would come to the training. People would think I was crazy whenever I was walking in the rain. I'm not the most patient person and never have been. I refused to let rain stop me, even if I didn't have a jacket. I eventually did start carrying a rain jacket in my backpack everywhere I went during rainy season, but before that I could be seen wearing my moto helmet while walking down the road to keep my head dry. I was definitely the crazy American a few times as a result but I didn't like the idea of waiting around not knowing if it was a storm that was going to last for ten minutes or a few hours, especially when I was trying to get home. I also hate being late to meetings so even though I was 100 percent positive that not a single person was going to show up to my meeting in the rain, I refused to risk being late just in case one person did decide to show up. One time I made the three-mile hike to the market in the rain, sliding along in the mud the entire way, just to have to wait for the rain to stop to catch a moto to take me the rest of the way. When I did get there, I still ended up waiting at the meeting place for over two hours, with participants blaming the rain even though it had ended much earlier. Another time I had already started walking when a downpour began. I had a jacket packed in my bag and I put it on thinking about how smart I was as I kept walking. It only took a few minutes for the water to seep into my shirt underneath and for my pants to be absolutely drenched. After that I still had to finish my walk to market, catch a moto to the agriculture school, and give a training before I could even consider changing my soggy, muddy clothes.

I also had to worry about the rain any time I travelled out of village. If I was caught in the rain while I was in Bafoussam or in Dschang, there was no way I was getting home anytime soon. Why? Because people refused to leave their houses in the rain. I could be sitting in a car or bus but it simply would not fill up because there was nobody coming. Nobody coming meant that it wouldn't leave, because instead of leaving at a scheduled time, the bus would not leave until it was full. Even when I was in Baleveng I had to move fast, since most moto men scattered when the rain started. I can only assume they figured that there would be no business once the rain started and that there was no point in sitting around the marketplace. I consider myself lucky that I never got stuck having to hike back up the hills to my house. There would be moto drivers who would refuse to take me, and I sometimes had to wait a bit, but I was always able to get a ride back. To avoid the problem I would do my best to be home by 1:00 pm, which was when the rain would almost always start. If I was at market still when I saw the rainclouds coming in or heard thunder, I would race to the motos to try and beat the rain home. I once even abruptly ending a meeting with the King when I heard a rumble of thunder from his palace salon; luckily he was understanding of my plight.

These challenges would continue even after the rain was over, simply because the roads were terribly muddy. The cost to go back up to my house doubled during and after the rain because the roads would get so slick. Sometimes I would have to get off the moto and walk up the steeper hills because the moto's tires would spin in the mud if there was too much weight on the bike. While annoying, it was sometimes entertaining to watch the bike still continue to struggle as it went up the hill. Meanwhile, I was trying very hard to not fall flat on my face in the mud. Plus, these rides took much longer once the roads got wet. There was one moto ride in particular where it took over 30 minutes, nearly three times as long as it takes when the roads were dry. Many of my rainy-day moto rides took a long time but I consider myself lucky that I was never on a moto that fell in the mud, as I know of a few volunteers that suffered who rather disgusting fate. When I was trying to get to a morning meeting after a night of rain, there was no chance of catching a moto. I would have to literally slide my way to the market. The downhills were as much of a struggle as the uphills. I would inevitably start sliding, and if I tried to take a step to catch my balance I would get very close to falling down completely. Instead, I would essentially surf my way until the slide stopped, and then start walking again.

One thing that the rain brought that could not be protected from, whether by proper clothing or timing of leaving the house, was mold. There was so much humidity in the air that there was nothing I could do to avoid the issue completely. My food was well protected because of the steps I had taken to avoid the mice, but the rest of my stuff was not. It mostly attacked my clothes. The clothes in the bottom of the boxes that I kept them in would get moldy, forcing me to do laundry for clothes that I hadn't even worn since the last time I washed them. The mold even got into my suitcase, which I was using to store things that I didn't use there but wanted at home. The two items that got completely destroyed were a weather wallet I had purchased at an artisan market and a leather bracelet I had purchased on vacation.

These inconveniences were not the biggest problems that rainy season brought. The biggest problem was standing water. Mosquitos breed in standing water, resulting in a boom to the local mosquito population when the rains returned. This meant a sharp rise in the rate of malaria for those in village. For me, this just meant a lot more bug bites, especially on my hands and feet. I was privileged to be able to take a daily prophylaxis and sleep under a mosquito net, both provided by the Peace Corps. Malaria was one of the biggest health problems that people in Baleveng faced. It was not taken as seriously because people exposed to it do eventually develop some antibodies to it. Nevertheless, they were one bad case of malaria away from dying. It is a disease that kills regardless of age, gender, or race.

Malaria's fatality rate is directly tied to socio-economic status. Simply put, those who can afford the treatment are much less likely to die from it. A malaria rapid test was around 500 CFA (the monetary unit of Cameroon), or a little bit less than a dollar, and the treatment for malaria at its early stages was similarly priced. But most villagers simply couldn't pay for it. They would say that it wasn't worth the test if it was likely something else. But during the few days that they would wait to see if their fever went away to avoid paying for a test that might turn out negative, the disease, if they had it, was getting worse. It was reproducing in their liver and then leaving to attack red blood cells. Villagers would go to the hospital a few days later, and while the test would cost the same, the treatment would dramatically increase if in fact it was malaria. My French tutor's son waited three days to get treatment, and it was 70 times more expensive because he needed several transfusions to replace the destroyed red blood cells in his system. People with severe enough cases of malaria need blood transfusions in order to survive and those do not come cheap. There is no "I owe you" for treatment. There is no health insurance. You need to pay for your treatment up front. Those who couldn't pay usually were able to borrow from others or ask for help from family or even from their quarter chief. But getting malaria treatment usually meant that they would have to sacrifice something else, whether it be the education for one of their children or the ability to buy vegetables at the market. It was definitely difficult to watch knowing that I would never have to worry about that since I was taking my prophylaxis daily and sleeping under a bed net every night. I also knew that that the long-standing habits of those in village were very difficult to change, like people keeping malaria nets in empty suitcases or using them for soccer nets.

While it was nice to not have to deal with the Massachusetts winter for two years, I did end up missing the four season cycle more than I thought I would. I missed the colors of the leaves changing and the feeling of that first warm spring day, even if it was followed by another week of chilly rain. Still, I enjoyed the predictability of the seasons in Cameroon rather than having to trust a large rodent to tell me how much more winter there would be that year.

As is similar around the world, I could feel the effects of global warming. I mentioned that my first dry season started a few weeks early. My second rainy season kept having fits. First, we had a full week of rain every day in early February, and then nothing until the middle of March. We had rain every other day for a few weeks and then in April we had minimal rain. Farmers planted once the rains came back in the middle of March, thinking that it was going to rain every day like it did almost every year prior. Then in August it simply stopped raining, and didn't come back for a month. Everyone had a lower crop yield as a result and the lack of rain was almost always the topic of conversations had at that time. You could hear the thunder and feel the vicious winds of storms passing by but no rain falling, and you could feel it in the humidity in the air. The day could be sunny but also have a 95% humidity rate and still not rain that day.

In the United States, we see the effects of global warming, such as the polar vortex, the melting of the ice caps and the resulting rising of the sea levels, and higher intensity of storms. These signs are alarming, but it was truly eye-opening to see how greatly global warming impacted those who were my neighbors and friends for two years. They cannot plant during the dry season, putting their livelihood at risk if the dry season keeps getting longer and longer. I left after two years, but those still there will be having to deal with the effects of global warming for years to come. These are all farmers living hand-to-mouth, and they are not in a position to adapt to rapid climate changes. They are worried whenever the weather doesn't follow the patterns that it has for their entire lifetime, and it is only going to get worse.

10

While I did obsess about almost every facet of life that I could
think of before departing for Cameroon, I hadn't thought
too much about travel and transportation. I don't remember
exactly why I didn't scour blogs for such information.
Perhaps it was that I was unable to truly find that much about
it. I found a lot of information about which places were the
best to go to, such as the beaches of Limbe and Kribe, Mount
Cameroon, and the cities of Yaoundé and Douala but almost
nothing about getting from point A to point B. It is probably
for the better that I didn't know enough to worry about it.

Travel was difficult at best. First of all, getting anywhere
involved going the three miles to the market. The walk
was downhill down a single dirt road for the majority of
the way, before turning and climbing up a large uphill to
finish the hike. Motos did not frequently pass me as I made
the hike, and if they did people were usually already on
them. Cameroon is one of the few countries that allows

its volunteers to ride on motos as long as they follow two conditions: they wear their Peace Corps issued helmet and they are the only passenger on the moto. All of the drivers thought that I loved to hike because I would always refuse their offer to hop on behind their other passengers. Additionally, these drivers could not be relied on to come to my house quickly when I needed a ride. The one time I needed to go to the hospital, I called four drivers and while all of them answered their phones, each refused to pick me up. Another time I called for one because I was in a rush, and it took an hour for him to get to my house; I could have walked to the market faster. During the school year I could time my hike to catch a ride down to the market as drivers were returning after dropping teachers off for their schooldays. This meant leaving my house at 7:30 a.m. which was not always the most convenient, and even then I could not assume that an empty moto was going to pass me by. Hard as they were to catch, I will never forget being on the back of a moto cruising through the mountainside on bumpy dirt roads that flooded easily.

The bigger issue with transit was that there was no such thing as personal space. Cars meant for four passengers carried as many as ten (if there were some children) and wouldn't leave unless they had at least six full sized adult passengers. This meant four passengers in the back, two passengers in the front seat, and sometimes even a "petite chauffeur" in the front seat with the driver as a seventh passenger. Depending on the driver's preference, the petite chauffeur could sit squished on the door side or part way onto the center console. I was once the petite chauffeur in the second case, with my head bent for the hour long drive as the driver kept reaching over me to change gears.

"Coasters" — smaller buses that had a single side aisle with jump seats that folded down to block it — were similarly crammed, with rows that could comfortably fit three stuffed full with five people. The bigger buses with a center aisle and rows of two seats on one side and three on the other were no more comfortable. The number of people per seat was correct but the size of the seat was too small for an adult of any size. I would look up at passengers getting on hoping that a small person would sit next to me instead of a big man or a mama with wide hips that would squish me into the wall of my hard fought window seat. Those window seats were too valuable to give up, since nobody else would open the windows on these buses and blowing air was my only comfort. People would in fact reach across my face to shut my window, but I'd stare at them as I opened it back up again.

After two years of traveling like this, I got jaded to it. Early on in my service, I realized that traveling around really was not worth that much effort. Many of the tourist places were in areas of the country that were restricted due to a multitude of issues including Boko Haram, the Anglophone Crisis, and unrest in the Central African Republic. To travel to the two biggest cities, which had more amenities, we had to get special permission and needed to have a very good reason to be going there for any chance at approval. It was for our own security and I completely agreed with the reasoning; as white people we always stood out, but in cities we became bigger targets for muggings by the virtue of the color of our skin. Even if I had been cleared, to me most places were too far out of village for me to have any desire to go. I preferred my simple village life to the stress of traveling.

To go anywhere that was not in the West, I would have to travel through Yaoundé. I did it countless of times for trainings and less so for vacation. It was a long and painful journey to Yaoundé. On my best travel day it took me seven hours and on the worst it took me over twelve hours. I would leave my house at 6:00 a.m. with my neighbor Joseph driving me on his moto to the market. He was the only driver to show up on time to pick me up, and that was only because I made sure that I hitched a ride with him while he was riding to the market to start looking for other fares. From the market area I had two options: I could buy a bus ticket or I could hitchhike to Bafoussam, our regional capital en route to Yaoundé.

My first few times traveling to Yaoundé I chose the bus that left from the Baleveng market. I had to go there first thing in the morning to buy my ticket and then I would wait for two to four hours (or more) for it to fill up and leave. It was the least comfortable and the slowest method of travel. It was the slowest for two main reasons. The first was that as the biggest option it just couldn't move as fast as other modes of transportation. The second was that we would have to stop at every single military and police checkpoint, of which there were many. When using other modes of transportation you can skip some, but the big buses were always stopped because with more passengers on board, there was a higher likelihood that someone was a threat. Additionally, the biggest modes of transportation served as the biggest opportunities for greedy military members and policemen. At these stops the moto boy, a person who stands by the door in all buses and helps get bags on and off the bus, was responsible for taking the passenger list and speaking with the gendarme. Usually some money was stuck into the passenger list for the gendarme to let us go quickly. But other times all of the passengers were forced to show their Cameroon National ID cards for the bus to continue. If there were passengers who did not have the proper identification, we were stuck at the checkpoint for at least a half an hour as the people who didn't have IDs sorted out their fines or bribes. I never understood why they would allow people to buy the ticket at the agency if they didn't have the proper identification, but I suppose the person selling the tickets wasn't the person dealing with the gendarmes. I also never understood when we had to wait for people who did have their identification but had to dig it out of their bags. Getting stopped for the IDs was nothing new, and when we first travel on our own during training we are told to make sure to have it on our person to make the check go more quickly. But inevitably there are people who have it deep in their bags. One time we were stopped and the woman next to me had left her identification in her big bag, which was being stored on top of the bus. They had to find the bag under the bags of almost every other passenger and bring it down for her to dig through to find the identification. Then when their IDs get checked everyone puts it back where it was, as if we aren't going to hit another checkpoint that will ask for their ID another hour down the road. Let's just say that my patience always grew thin as we got closer to Yaoundé and hit more and more checkpoints that secure the city.

Whenever the buses were stopped, either to pay tolls or to deal with gendarmes, people selling food and drink would flock to the windows to make some money. The bus would heat up quickly while stopped with so many people on board, so people would finally open the windows. The vendors would stick their hands in the open windows to show off the kola nuts, peanuts, or candies that they had for sale. Sometimes the bus would start moving again in the middle of a transaction, and the vendor would run alongside the bus to make sure the passenger got the food before money was thrown out the window for the vendor to collect, since the bus waits for nobody.

On these long, crowded journeys, there is nothing to do but sit there, stuck with someone's elbows going into your ribs or your legs crammed together, except ride it out. One time the woman next to me was holding a young child, no more than a one year old. I had my bag in my own lap since there was nowhere else to put it, and I was doing my best to simply focus on ignoring the numbness of my butt and the heat I was feeling since everybody refused to open any windows. All of the sudden, I had baby vomit on my bag. By the time I noticed what was happening, the baby was getting sick in it's mother's lap. She asked the driver to stop so that she could get cleaned up, but the driver refused. While stuck bunched together, she had a lap full of baby vomit and I had some on my bag, and there was absolutely nothing that either of us could really do. She took the now disgusting sweater off of the baby and used it to wipe off my bag and her lap, but it had nowhere to go except onto the floor. She couldn't properly clean herself until the driver decided to take a break a few hours later. Before that moment, I always thought it was a bit silly how one of the bus rules was no vomiting. Painted in French on the upper walls of most coasters was a notice: 'No smoking, no vomiting, no fighting... we are not responsible for baggage that is not paid for.' I found out that if you get sick, that bus is not stopping and you're just going to have to deal with it. Just as the bus didn't wait for vendors, they were not going to stop for one person's problems.

No matter which mode of transportation I took to get to Yaoundé, I always got anxious as we got into the city. We would enter the city limits but it would be another 45 minutes to an hour before I knocked on the gate of the transit house (a small house in Yaoundé owned by Peace Corps for volunteers passing through the capital) asking to be let in by the guard. The bus or coaster would seemingly crawl as people asked to be let off, and then we had to wait for their bags to be brought down from the roof or out of the luggage compartment. During one particularly long trip I had already been traveling for over 12 hours and the sun was about to set. We got to Yaoundé and had been slogging our way through when a taxi hit our bus. It wasn't a normal accident, during which people would yell at each other for a minute or two before driving off. In this accident, the taxi got stuck in the wheel well of the bus. People ended up getting out of the taxi and others from the bus got off to actually lift the taxi out of the wheel well to enable both vehicles to keep going as if nothing happened. After 12 hours of travel, not even that sight fazed me: I was focused on the transit house, a shower, and a hot meal from the pizza place next door. I was antsy to get to my destination so I got off at the next stop to depot a taxi to my end destination. I was paying more, but the rest of the ride was much faster and I had the taxi to myself.

If you want to travel all of the way to the Adamawa region in the Grand North of Cameroon, you have to take the overnight train for at least 15 hours from Yaoundé. I took this trip up and back for New Years 2019. To do this, I had to complete the previously described long travel day to Yaoundé and then spend the next day waiting until it was time to head to the train station. The train left at 7:00 p.m. and, given my history of traveling to Yaoundé, I couldn't risk attempting to make the trip all in one day. The train ride up to the Adamawa region was eventful to say the least. I had purchased a seat in first class, one of three classes of seats, ahead of time. First class, the middle of the three classes, means that I was assigned a seat and that it had leg room. In second class, the seats are first come first serve; if you don't get a seat you have to spend the entire train ride standing. The sleeper car, which I took on the way back down, has small cabins of two sets of bunk beds, all of which are assigned.

I got to the station way too early. I sat and waited for the train to arrive, and finally headed to the train when they opened the platform to passengers. I got to my seat and the one next to me was empty. As much as I wished for the seat to stay empty, luck was not on my side. A random man came and put his bag in the seat next to me before going outside. As the night went on, he was rarely ever in the seat and was in other cars drinking. At one point, he got into fights with people in other cars as the train workers realized that he did not actually have a first class ticket. When he had the same fight again in our car, he ripped off his shirt to fight people, claiming that he belonged in the first-class car. The fight moved back another car and he never returned — a policeman returned to grab his bag. For the rest of the overnight ride, I had the small row to myself. This small improvement did not mean it was comfortable, and I barely slept that night. We kept having to stop at stations and the cars would get stuffy since we were rolling through the hot jungles of the East region. At these stops, just like at the check points on the highway to and from Yaoundé, people would swarm the windows trying to sell food and drink to passengers. Eventually as the sun rose, we left the jungle and entered the savannah that makes up the Adamawa region, which meant that we still had at least four hours to go. On the way back I took the sleeper car, and I still don't quite know why that wasn't recommended to me in the first place because that was one of the best travel experiences I had in Cameroon. The beds were assigned, and since I got a top bunk I didn't have to deal with people climbing over me. Overall, I was very lucky with my train rides. I have heard horror stories from other volunteers who had rides that lasted nearly 20 hours, stuck at the same station for hours on end, leaving the passengers sweltering throughout the night while getting attacked by bugs.

While transportation became one of my biggest challenges, with even "quick trips to Dschang" involving either a three-mile hike or moto ride along with a 20 minute cab ride stuffed in like a circus clown, I'll admit that at first there was a sense of novelty to these challenges. During training, the 20 members of my agriculture stage would laugh as we stuffed ourselves into small coasters. While pretty soon I became a pro at moto rides, I will never forget my first ride through the roads on the way to the center of Banganté during my first week of training. I was absolutely petrified at first, clutching the luggage rack behind me as if I was going to fall off at any moment. It took awhile for me to get sufficiently comfortable to at least loosen my grip enough to stop feeling the shake of the engine in my arms. It was a beautiful ride through the rolling hills, and I loved the feeling of the wind whipping against my face when I opened up my visor to keep it from fogging up. That was my favorite part of moto rides, and the only times I would ever close my visor were either during dry seasons when cars or when motos would kick up big clouds of dust or it was raining as I was trying to race home.

One of the eeriest parts of riding a moto, which was actually true of almost every form of transportation I used in Cameroon, was that the drivers would turn off the engine when going downhill. The idea was that it would save gas; it was a wide-held belief that the ten seconds of an engine being off saved more gas than was used when turning the motor back on. At the bottom of the hill, if you were on a moto, you would have to remember to hold on tight to avoid slamming your helmet into the driver's head as he rapidly slowed down to turn the moto back on. I must have done that hundreds of times during my time in Cameroon, not just when the motos were turned back on but also when the drivers unexpectedly braked for a speed bump that they didn't see or when they were having difficulty changing gears going up a hill.

Pretty soon, moto rides became a part of my daily life and I came to enjoy the ride back to my house at the end of a long day. The drivers at the market knew where my house was and sometimes I didn't even have to say a word except thank you when I paid them upon arrival at my house. I also used motos to avoid traffic in Bafoussam. Though they were a more expensive way to get around, they would whip around cars stuck in traffic and, unlike in those cars with their many passengers, you had space to yourself. While it had become routine, nothing is ever guaranteed to be smooth during a Peace Corps service. Twice I was on a moto and we ran out of gas. Both times, the driver had me get off so that he could flip the bike over and slosh gas around enough to give the engine enough life for us to get to our destination. The second time, this trick got us closer but we didn't make it. I had to walk the rest of the way. There were times that drivers would stop under a big tree instead of driving in the rain, and other times we would go slowly on the slick muddy roads through the downpour. I learned to take my phone out of my pocket and put it into a small plastic bag that I kept in my backpack throughout the rainy season because I would arrive home completely soaked. There were also two times when I was involved in minor moto accidents. Once I was flung off the moto because the driver missed the turn and tried to take it too sharp and fast, causing his tire to skid in the dust. Luckily it was a dirt road and I wasn't injured. In my second accident, I was in Bafoussam darting through traffic when another moto collided into us. My leg got pinched between the two motos. Luckily since neither moto was going very fast in the heavy traffic, I ended up being fine.

What I learned through all of the difficulties traveling was to let go a bit. I am very schedule-oriented, and it was tough to let go of that. Not knowing when I was going to arrive somewhere, having my estimated time of arrival tick past, or even being late to meetings because the car didn't have enough passengers yet would drive me insane. It forced me to leave obscenely early for meetings or, for longer travel, to simply not plan on what time I would actually arrive. While not something I was able to achieve every time, I taught myself to breathe and to relinquish control. I would get there when I got there, and no amount of stressing out or hoping that I would get there sooner would actually get me there any faster. Similar to how nothing would work but everything would work out, I would never get somewhere when I wanted to but I would always get there eventually. I would like to think that it has helped me improve my patience as well as to be more cognizant of what things are out of my control. But I suppose I will have to wait to see if that lesson sticks.

11

Simply because life feels harder when living in a rural village, getting sick or hurt felt like the sky was falling. It didn't help that there was no immediate medical care except for a phone call to the Peace Corps Medical Office (PCMO). I tried to be thankful every day that I woke up and went to bed with no medical problem causing any issues that day. Most days that was the case, and I was very lucky. But there were days that felt like the end of the world. It was during those days that I would question what I was still doing in Cameroon, as I sat alone in my house without someone right there to take care of me or even just to commiserate with me. Unlike in other Peace Corps countries, and unlike during my training period, Cameroon volunteers do not live in houses with a family. As a proud independent person as well as an introvert, I never called someone to come keep me company or take care of me. The only thing I really could do was call PCMO, text with fellow volunteers, and wait it out. Several times I had to make the trip to the nearest pharmacy, which was all the way in Dschang. I definitely missed having a CVS or a Walgreens within a ten-minute drive from home. Even if there had been someone I would have asked to go to the pharmacy for me, I needed to be there in case they didn't have what I needed. In that case I would have to call PCMO again to give me alternatives or even put them on the phone with the pharmacist.

But like I said, I was lucky. I was not sick too often, or at least not as often as other volunteers were. I only had to go to Yaoundé twice for a medical reasons, and those were for a tetanus shot and a skin biopsy when I was feeling fine. I can't imagine making the travel from Baleveng to Yaoundé while feeling terrible. Additionally, and this may seem strange but other volunteers from all over the world will know what I'm talking about, I never double dragonned. A double dragon is when you get sick to your stomach in both directions at the same time. For me, it was a point of pride that I could say that I never actually even vomited in Cameroon. I knocked on wood every time I mentioned it since I knew that my turn could easily come. But when you simplify your diet due to your lack of cooking skills and you are very careful about foods that others give you, your stomach stays happier. One of my tricks was to carry a big ziplock bag with me. If I didn't like the look of the food, I would tell people I wasn't hungry but that I would guard it for later. I would give it to Pa Thomas who was always thankful. This strategy prevented anyone from being insulted, and it kept both Pa Thomas and my stomach happy.

I was very careful throughout my time to drink only filtered water or unopened water. The vendors along the highway sold cold water. It was tempting, especially on those cramped buses with little air flow, but it was important to know that this water was not actually filtered. The bottles had been filled at a river or from a well and placed in a refrigerator somewhere. I had no way of knowing the quality of the water, or if there were any parasites in it, just by looking at it. I could only be sure by either filtering the water myself and bringing it with me or by buying it at a boutique and making sure the seal had not been broken. I filled up my water filter with five liters of water almost every day and would carry a liter with me whenever I left my house.

But no matter how careful I was with what I ate, sometimes my stomach revolted. The first time this happened, I was coming back from my first conference after being in village for three months. My entire stage was put up in a hotel in Ebolowa, the capital city of the South region, for a few weeks to get more training based on what we had found our villages truly needed, plus to enjoy some good food and hot showers. When I got to the bus station to head back to Yaoundé, I felt nauseated to the point that I thought I would get sick. On the entire three-hour long bus ride cramped in a coaster bus, my body ached terribly. I thought it was from the South region's famed humidity that I had been avoiding with the air conditioning in our hotel. When we finally got to Yaoundé, I learned had a fever — and it kept rising. When it hit over 101 degrees Fahrenheit that night, I called PCMO. Whenever anyone has a fever the first step is to take a rapid malaria test, since it is possible to get malaria even if you never miss a prophylaxis dose and sleep under a mosquito net. A visit to PCMO and a stool sample told that I had amoebic dysentery. While I don't want to go into too much information on my symptoms, I can say that I now understand how dysentery can kill people. School-age children playing Oregon Trail laugh when someone dies of it, but I have a new respect for it. I was stuck in the transit house for a week, unable to travel the full day back to post simply because I couldn't go that long without having to use the bathroom, and I wasn't alone. Two other people in my stage also fell sick with amoebic dysentery, making it was fairly clear that we all got sick from the food at the hotel. While it was not fun to have to get up every 30 minutes to use the restroom, it was a lot better to be stuck in the transit house with the self-dubbed Amoeba Squad than to be that sick alone in village.

Amazingly enough, that bout of amoebic dysentery was not the worst I felt in my entire service. I think that I felt worse both physically and psychologically when I got the flu six months later, largely because I was alone. There was nobody else to entertain me as I was stuck in bed with another high fever, unable to breathe through my nose and constantly coughing. I barely had any food in the house and I didn't have the energy to go to the market. I had site visitors, two trainees who were at the halfway point of their training period, coming a few days later when I still wasn't well. I had to get the three miles to the market to pick them up since they had never been to my house before. I almost fell off of the moto since I didn't have the energy to stay alert. But at least when they arrived at my house I had people to keep me company for a bit, even if it was them sitting on my bedroom floor peppering me with questions about life as a volunteer while I laid in bed. I'm sure it wasn't the beginning to site visit week that they were looking for.

Though I did not get sick too often, I sometimes wondered if PCMO ever thought that I was a threat to myself given how many times I texted them with pictures of slices and burns. I sliced my hand with a machete several times because I was too tired to focus and wasn't paying attention. I am thankful that I was wearing gloves each time, protecting my hands from much worse injuries. I used those gloves for the rest of my service, getting my left hand very dirty simply because of the holes in it. Torn as they were, the gloves treated me well, and I knew that they would continue to protect my hands as I worked. I also burned my hand on several occasions while cooking, the stupider one being from when I didn't think that the pot cover sitting next to the burner would be hot.

The worst hand injury I had, however, was no fault of my own. I was weeding my farm when a rusty cane rat trap someone had buried on my farm shut on my hand. My hand, digging to make sure I was taking out the weeds by the roots, set off the trap. I wish I was kidding. But I was lucky. It only caught my middle finger at the top joint because I was able to yank my hand out of the way in time, and even then my finger was not trapped completely. My finger caught one of the nails that are meant for piercing the neck of the cane rat but slipped it off before the bar closed. I did have to go to the hospital in Dschang to get it professionally cleaned out and covered before visiting PCMO in Yaoundé for a tetanus shot. Horrible as it was, I do not consider having to travel to the hospital and to Yaoundé as bad luck. When I asked Angilbert about the hidden rat trap upon my return, he told me that I was not the first victim of them. They are set by people looking to make some money at the market, and those people don't care whose land they bury them on. Another woman he knew lost half of her foot after stepping on one, so it is easy to consider my situation as good luck.

Additionally, as in the case of almost any Peace Corps service, bugs could be a huge health risk. There were always a ton of insects in my house and even though I had a mosquito net, I spent a lot of time on my balcony or on my couch without such protection. My preference for open window seats when traveling and leaving my moto helmet visor open also created points of entry for bugs. I once noticed a bee inside my helmet while we were driving. It took all of my effort to not freak out and tip the bike over, instead choosing to slowly try and flick it out. Another time while traveling, a bug bit me near my eye, or at least that was my theory after waking up one morning with my right eye swollen shut.

I had to go give a tree grafting training on that first day, and then afterwards make the trip to the Dschang pharmacy and back before it started to rain. Another week my lip was randomly swollen, making it difficult to eat, and I could only assume it was some sort of insect bite. Yet another time I had a swollen toe resulting from a chigger. Chiggers are bugs that dig into people's feet to lay eggs. I usually avoided the issue altogether by wearing my hiking shoes almost every day. That day, however, I happened to be wearing a dress and chose to wear my Chacos instead of closed toed shoes. I took a muddy shortcut and of course one of the only times I didn't wear closed toed shoes, a chigger found its way in. I didn't realize it until a few days later when I was visiting another volunteer, and thankfully she agreed to expertly dig it out with a needle.

The final seemingly omnipresent health challenge was dermatology. Early in my time at post I got a hole in the bottom of my foot from a pebble. The skin grew very weirdly in its place and I didn't think anything of it, since it wasn't painful, until my dad and sister came to visit me. I decided to show it to them. They said it could be a wart and that I definitely needed to get it checked out. Of course, they were right. The dermatologist came to the medical office the next time I was in the transit house and burned it off with liquid nitrogen. Nothing hurt worse than the needle going deep into the pad of my foot to numb it for the nitrogen. The foot throbbed from the burn for days. But three weeks later, once the small blister was gone, the wart grew back.

The next time I went to Yaoundé I had to go through it all again, except this time they burned the foot for much longer and over a much wider area. The next day I had a quarter sized blister on my foot raised a full centimeter that made it nearly impossible to walk. That night the foot swelled up in reaction to the much more serious burn and I thought I had an infection. I had to wait in the transit house for the weekend before seeing the dermatologist again to make sure it was done properly this time. He lanced the blister and sent me back to village that day. It took over another week for it to stop leaking, and another month for me to be able to walk properly, leading to a lot of money spent on motos and more time than usual spent inside my house.

I think that the recovery from the blister removal was one of the lowest parts of my service. I am someone who uses exercise as a coping mechanism, and often used the three-mile hikes to the market to sort out my thoughts. It was a stressful month for me since I was also studying for the law school admissions test at the time, and not having one of my major coping mechanisms led to stress-induced eczema to breaking out on my hands. I had it occasionally earlier in my service on a finger and it usually went away after a few days. This time it was on several fingers on both hands, and felt like it was spreading to other fingers every day. I called PCMO and they sent me back to the pharmacy in Dschang, yet again, to pick up a corticosteroid. My eczema continued to come back periodically throughout the rest of my service but I was able to use the cream I had already purchased which greatly helped reduce the symptoms.

It was during the low time of both the wart issue and the eczema that I did a mental health evaluation with PMCO and almost got a counselor. My anxiety was at its highest point during that time and while I always had trouble sleeping while in Cameroon, it was exceptionally difficult to sleep then. I was getting angry almost daily at small things that I usually could handle with ease, like my phone service going out during a call or getting interrupted during my morning meditation. When my foot finally got better I was able to bring back my routines. I started working out almost every day. I could hike all of the way to the market. I could do my farm work and not stress about what needed to be done but couldn't actually get done. I continued to use my other coping mechanisms like meditation, journaling, and calling my dad almost daily. But there was something about my foot finally becoming better that calmed my anxiety and my anger at that point in time. My mental health was never consistent during my service. I could be having a perfect day and somehow at night stay up wondering if I could survive the next 200 or 300 days there. During low times, I was my own life coach. I told myself that I had been through downs before. I told myself that my reactions were normal, and that I had gotten through worse things before. During the second half of my service I would tell myself that I had already made it through more than how many days I had left, meaning that there was no reason why I wouldn't be able to make it to close of service.

When I had less than two months left, I stopped doubting that I would make it to the end of my service. Of course, with that mentality I faced yet another major skin issue that made me start questioning myself again. It was then that I noticed an intermittent sharp tingling pain in my leg. It had happened before but it was becoming more and more frequent, and lasting longer. It finally happened to me while I was home instead of out, and I lifted up my pant leg to massage it. That was when I finally noticed a brand new abnormal looking mole, directly above the pain. I realized that it could be skin cancer, and called PCMO. We went through the ABC's of skin cancer symptoms, and they decided to have me come to Yaoundé to get a biopsy.

When I got to Yaoundé, I was at first told that I would not actually be able to get the biopsy done in Cameroon. I would have to be medically separated from the Peace Corps just to get the test done. My mind went into hyperdrive as we waited for the dermatologist to show up. I didn't want to get sent home to get a test done, leaving without having a chance to say goodbye to those that had become my family, and then learn that it wasn't actually skin cancer. But luckily the dermatologist brought the tools to do a punch biopsy and convinced PCMO to let me get it done. She numbed my leg before pushing the circular razor blade 4-5 millimeters deep into my skin layers to pull out a chunk to send to the lab for examination. Then, after stitching up the hole, she told me that I would not get the results for three weeks. While most people would be more anxious to get the results sooner, I breathed a sigh of relief. It gave me three full weeks to prepare those in my village for the possibility that I would have to be leaving early. I hoped for the best but expected the worst, and started to believe that my results would come back positive. Luckily, I was wrong yet again. Exactly three weeks later I got a phone call saying that the results had come back negative for skin cancer and that I didn't have to worry about not finishing up the remaining three weeks of my service.

Up until the very end, I pushed through all of the health issues. These were not just physical but also the mental. There is a sense of surviving a Peace Corps service, and I can proudly say that I did. I don't think that I came out a stronger person, just as someone who better knows her own strengths. I tell myself that after being able to survive the physical and mental challenges of a Peace Corps service, I should be able to survive almost anything else life can throw at me.

12

The only thing I had ever grown before going to Cameroon was an aloe plant that my sister gave to me. I never had a green thumb, nor did I really care to make any effort to develop one. This was not a factor when I was switched to being an agriculture volunteer because I didn't have any health experience either. I was told that not all agriculture volunteers do farming. Some agriculture volunteers focus on the business side of agriculture work. Others do demonstrations and trainings without growing anything themselves. Others don't have their own farms but help out farmers at their farms. Finally, many volunteers have their own home gardens. I didn't know which category of agriculture volunteer I would fall into.

Somehow, I eventually ended up as a true Bamiléké farmer. I had a farm, a garden, and even chickens. This was the result of several factors. One factor was a desire to truly understand how the people of Baleveng lived. I figured that without that understanding it would be difficult to grasp their needs. For example, it is one thing to know that people's farms are miles away from their homes; it is another to experience hiking that distance home after a full day clearing land, or to make that trip six times with a bag full of harvested beanstalks on your head and get caught in the rain on the last trip. Another factor was my desire to learn, not just about the struggles but how agriculture is done there. It was a desire for some experiential learning, knowing that my chance to live in Baleveng was a once in a lifetime opportunity.

The Model Farm

My opportunity to have a farm ended up falling into my lap in my first few weeks in village. I was doing protocol, which is when a counterpart introduces a volunteer to local officials, with Angilbert. Together, the counterpart and the volunteer give the officials letters from the Peace Corps staff that help explain what the volunteer is doing and for how long they will be living there. Our last in this series of meetings was with the Chief of Banza, on a Saturday morning. He lived in Douala most of the time and would come back to village mainly for ceremonial events. He was back in village for a funeral, which gave us the opportunity to meet. With my then relatively low level of French and a lot of help from Angilbert, we discussed what I was hoping to accomplish and what he wanted out of an agriculture volunteer. One of his desires was a demonstration farm, and he offered nearly 500 square meters of his land that hadn't been farmed recently. On one hand, the dormant land meant that we would have to do a ton of work to clear it. On the other hand, it meant that not only were we not taking land from anyone else, but the soil would be rested and have a lot more nutrients.

Angilbert and I put a ton of work into that farm. It seemed like it took absolutely forever to finally clear it all that first year. We cleared it and burned the brush before turning the land and making row after row of garden beds. I will admit that Angilbert did almost all of the work of making the garden beds due to timing issues on my end. In our first year, the time for making garden beds was when I was at training for a month and in my second year, it was when I had foot issues from the wart. Even after he made the garden beds the first year, my extended absence from village made me miss the first planting season. We had to wait until August to try again because farming needs to follow the seasonal calendar. The garden beds were done and we could leave them there, but that meant that I spent about an entire week clearing the land of new weeds so we could plant.

That first year, the farm did not produce well. The large black crows with white chests that flew around our village had eaten all of the corn that I had planted because we didn't put down the ash that deters them. I also wanted to attempt to plant soy. Soy has many nutritional benefits, especially for a community where meat is relatively expensive. I wanted to show that it could be grown and hopefully encourage others to do the same. However, I learned that there was a reason why nobody in my village grew soy — it didn't grow well. We had almost no soy to harvest.

It was definitely a frustrating first farming year. Part of that was because I didn't really know what I was doing and part of it was my determination to follow my own plans. If I had talked further with Angilbert about it, I would have learned that soy simply doesn't grow well in Banza. Instead, I just assumed that there was a pivot opportunity. Eleanor Roosevelt once said, "Learn from the mistakes of others. You can't live long enough to make them all yourself." I missed the opportunity to do that by not asking enough questions before the first time we planted.

As frustrating as the first farming year was, the second year was a huge success. We were able to complete two planting seasons. I learned significantly more as a result and also felt a lot more pride because I did almost all of the work on my own. Angilbert helped guide me but I did almost everything on my own except making the garden beds. As a result, I learned that the first planting season depends entirely on the rain. People prepare their land in February and March, and then plant as soon as the rains come. In 2019, we didn't plant until almost the end of March because that was when the rains came. Planting was simple: I took a short machete and stuck it in the ground to make a small opening, dropped some seeds in, and covered it back up before taking a step forward to repeat the process. The only difference was the spacing between each step — the beans were planted much closer together and on either side of the garden bed while the corn was planted further apart and down the middle. Corn and beans are often planted together, in Cameroon and around the world, because the beanstalks grow up the corn stalks. Even with free standing beanstalks, this practice is encouraged because beans put much needed nitrogen back into the soil. While we did not do this on my farm, people also usually planted a cover crop, such as peanuts or squash, to suppress the growth of weeds.

While most farms in the area focused primarily on corn production, the beans were our main production goal. We did plant an improved corn variety but that was because it took almost zero extra effort to do so. Between clearing the land and planting, I had gone to the Institute of Research for Agricultural Development (IRAD) station in Dschang to search for improved bean seeds. I purchased a kilo of them with the plan that if they were successful on the model farm, they could be distributed to farmers in Banza. In turn, those who received the free half kilogram of bean seeds would have to give the same quantity of seeds to five more people after they themselves reproduced it.

Something that I loved about farming, but which drove me crazy at times, was that it brought a lot of work at once and then long periods of waiting. After planting in March, one of those waiting periods arrived. We waited a month before weeding the plot again to keep the weeds from suffocating the beans. After another month of waiting, it was time to weed again. Some people left the weeds on their farm, but I chose not to. I saw that the beans were thriving and I wanted to give them optimal growing conditions.

Just a few weeks after my second time weeding, it was time to harvest our beans. I mistakenly thought was going to be the easiest part because I didn't think through a major step. After taking them out of the ground I had to somehow get them the mile back to my house. I brought two big empty 40 kilogram bags to put them in and thought that they couldn't be that heavy. Beanstalks are not heavy, at least not until you stuff hundreds of them into bags trying to take up every square centimeter of empty space. We used old banana leaves to shut the bags instead of tying the bags' corners to allow us to put just a few more stalks in.

I ended up having to take six trips with a bag full of beanstalks on my head over the course of two days. It could have been completed in one day but when I was on my way back to the farm for the third bag, already stuffed, it started to downpour. I was wearing a jacket but it was an onslaught that soaked my pants all the way through within minutes. It formed small but quick moving streams on the muddy walking path. But I couldn't turn around. I couldn't leave the third bag on the farm in the pouring rain since that could ruin the beans. Water makes roots start to come out of bean seeds, and if you don't plant them right after that happens, the seeds go bad. Instead of going back home, I continued on through the rain to the farm, put the bag on my head and walked my way back. The bag was even heavier waterlogged, and with an already tired neck I continuously was deciding whether to take a few more steps or to take a break in the rain. I ended up taking two breaks, since a few additional minutes in the rain wouldn't make a difference after already getting soaked.

The next morning I woke up to a sore neck and upper back. All I wanted to do was stay in bed all day but I couldn't since I had to do it all again. Luckily, it didn't rain. On the second day, I passed by a group of people preparing for a funeral, all stopping and staring at the crazy white girl walking by with a giant bag of beans on her head as if she thought she was a local. They didn't understand that I actually lived in Banza, and had for over 18 months. They wanted to stop me to take pictures of me and with me. It slowed me down, which my neck and back didn't enjoy, but in the end it all got done. I was able to create a giant pile of drying beans next to my chicken cage.

The end results were incredible. My one kilogram of beans turned into 17 kilograms. I used a very slow harvesting method to ensure that none of these were destroyed by fault of my own. In my first year, I had harvested two small garden beds of beans following the village method of tapping the pile of dried bean pods with a stick to break them open, allowing the seeds to fall below. Almost the entire batch got ruined by worms. Given all of the work I had put into the improved beans in my second attempt, I didn't want any to go bad. Instead of the quick and easy method, I was meticulous in how I harvested the improved beans. It took me four days rather than a single afternoon. I pulled all of the bean pods off of the stalks before opening them one by one. I did it this way because when opening them individually I could inspect them for worm damage. If there was a worm, I threw the damaged beans and worm off of my patio. If it was fine, I put it in a basin. There was a rhythm to it; I would open the bean pod onto the table, dumping the empty pod onto a separate pile. I would visually examine the beans while I did that and if I saw no damage, they were swept to the basin. While sweeping the beans I would grab the next bean pod to repeat the process. Once I was finally finished, I swept the entire patio to make sure there were no worms hiding, then put the beans in a pile where I had left the stalks a few days earlier to dry some more before putting them back into a bag to store until distribution.

I could have given out the beans as soon as they were ready, but I didn't want people to accidentally eat them. The plan was for them to eat the beans eventually but first I needed their help to reproduce them. My hope was that everyone in the village would receive the beans before people started to eat or sell them. At a 17:1 reproduction rate there should have been plenty to give away, but mold destroyed over half of my beans. After drying them, I had put them in a bag to protect them from mice when I went away on vacation. While I was gone, the rainy season mold attacked everything. With Angilbert's help I was able to recover the other half but I was only able to distribute to half as many people as I had planned. Even so, I look at the project with pride. I wish I could have been there to see more of the project as it unfolded, but unfortunately my time in

Cameroon finished just as it was time to harvest the beans during the second season. I ended up giving half of a kilogram of beans to 15 people who had signed a form I created saying they would give away the same quantity to five more people. I ended up going back to IRAD to purchase more beans for the King at his request, giving him four kilograms, and I saved the last kilogram to replant on the farm again in August during my last planting season in Cameroon. Following up with those farmers and doing further bean distributions became the responsibility of the next volunteer.

Similarly, later that season we were able to harvest our hybrid corn variety. Once again I walked the mile from my farm to my house loaded with crops. Since the corn was much heavier, I was unable to carry it on my head, instead carrying it in backpacks on my back and my stomach as well as a bag I hugged to my chest on top of the backpack on my stomach. The corn was a lot heavier but it only took two trips. When I got to my house, I removed the husks, picked out the bad kernels with a knife so they wouldn't contaminate the rest, and left it all out to dry for months. Then I removed the kernels from the cobs, put them in bags, and distributed the corn to 16 people in October, my final month in Cameroon.

The Garden

The garden was not a major project of mine. It was just two garden beds next to a well-used path near my house. The idea was that people would see the garden and hopefully be inspired to have home gardens of their own. I knew there really was not much I could accomplish with it from the perspective of changing behaviors. Any time I talked with farmers about having their own gardens, they told me they couldn't afford to use their land for something that doesn't sell well, even if it was for home nutrition. Instead, their lack of income forced them to use almost every piece of land for cash crops since that would bring in more money.

I still decided to start a small garden. I cleared the land, prepared the garden beds, and planted orange fleshed sweet potato vines that I got from a nearby volunteer. Orange fleshed sweet potatoes are nutritious, especially for those living with or caring for people with HIV. I had no idea what the HIV rates in Banza and Baleveng were, but I wanted to start to reproduce the vines to distribute to those in village since it was another opportunity to improve home nutrition. Sadly, my timing was terrible. I had gotten the vines from another volunteer a few months before dry season at the end of 2018, and the ones I planted didn't grow long enough to distribute to people living near streams who could water the vines during dry season. My vines completely dried out in the following months. I simply could not justify using 10 liters of water every day to water my sweet potatoes when there were times we didn't have enough water to drink. I chose to leave the tubers in the ground to see if they would re-sprout when the rains came back. While I don't know the science behind it, they did. I continued to grow the sweet potato vines during the rest of my service, but I was not very successful at it. However, I did not plant all of the vines that I had received from the other volunteer. I had given a few vines to the agricultural school and had completely forgotten about it until preparing my final report. I stopped by the school over a year after giving them the vines to see how many students received them. I was expecting between five and ten recipients. To my pleasant surprise, I learned that the school had planted the vines on site for reproduction, and had watered them all through dry season. All 40 students and staff members received the vines to grow in their quarters, and they gave away vines to an average of two more people each. In one visit I went from viewing my sweet potato project as a total failure to seeing it as a huge success, with at least 120 people receiving sweet potato vines.

When I realized that my own sweet potatoes were not going to grow well, my garden focus shifted away from having optimal conditions for vine reproduction and towards producing vegetables to eat and share with my neighbors. In the two garden beds already in use, I added manure before planting carrot and tomato seeds. When I went down to the garden again a few weeks later to inspect it, I saw that the tomatoes never germinated. I even tried planting them again in polypots kept next to my house to no avail. While I was disappointed about the tomatoes, my carrots grew in well. However, I planted them too late to reap the benefits. I told Pa Thomas that he could harvest them about a month or two after I left. While not turning out award winning vegetables,

I am proud of even being able to complete a garden given my lack of agriculture experience before arriving in Cameroon.

Livestock

When I arrived in Cameroon, I told myself I wasn't going to get any animals because I couldn't bring them back and I didn't want to leave any pets behind. I also figured that since I was out of Banza often for trainings and other events, it wasn't right to get any animals. But with six months left in my service I realized that I wanted to raise some farm animals. Part of it was because I wanted to complete my agricultural experience. After all, I had the farm and the garden already. I also planted two avocado trees on my landlord's property. The other part of it was that I wanted to raise them for my goodbye party. The goodbye party was thrown to thank my community for all that they had done for me during my two years, and as I learned through ceremonies the best way to do that is by feeding others. I figured it would be cheaper to buy three week old chicks and raise them than to buy adult chickens to cook. I also had an idea to get two goats, one for the party and one as a thank you gift specifically for the King. I ended up having to scrap these ideas. In terms of the goats, it was because I waited too long for a baby goat to grow big enough. There was also a goat disease at our market. I couldn't risk buying and giving away a sick adult goat that would get the King's other goats sick. For the chickens, people ended up wanting to buy them for reproduction in their concessions. I couldn't justify saying no to that so that I could eat them.

With the chickens I jumped off the deep end. At the end of May 2019, I went to the agriculture store at the market, which is an old shipping container with some chairs outside. I spoke with the owner, Vikeng Pierre, about my plans to buy six young chicks at the next market day. We talked for a while, discussing my plans for feed, water, vaccinations, and whether I wanted white chickens or village chickens. I learned that people selling chickens at the market will have already vaccinated them, and that white chickens will grow quicker than village chickens but village chickens have stronger immune systems. That day I ended up buying 25 kilograms of chicken feed, a cage, and a waterer. For the chicken feed we looked up the feed recipes for young chicks. The ingredients for the feed were individually measured and put into the bag, and I had to mix it by hand it after hauling it home.

I got to market day first thing the following morning. I wanted to get the best chickens available before any diseases swept through the market area. Pierre lent me a small carrier that I used to carry them from the back corner of the market to the main road where his store was located. As I was walking through the market with my empty chicken carrier, people kept stopping me to ask what I was doing. I used the opportunity to ask each of those people what I should be paying to keep from getting bamboozled by a good sounding yet white man price. As I was explaining that I was going to go buy chickens, someone I didn't know asked me if I was interested in village chickens or white chickens. His name was Tani, and he was selling village chickens. I chose to purchase from him. I had already decided I was going to buy village chickens for their stronger immune systems. Plus, since I met him before getting to the livestock section of market, I wouldn't have to choose among different vendors yelling at me to buy from them. I got a good price, I wasn't harassed, and the chickens didn't get sick.

While walking back to Pierre's, people stopped and stared at the crazy white girl again. Some asked me where I was planning on going with them, mistaking me for a tourist instead of someone who had been living just three miles from the market for a year and a half already. Though I had lived there for a long time, our market drew crowds of people from all over, many people whom I did not know. When I got to Pierre's, we put the chickens into the cage and I rode a moto back home with them in the cage behind me. The moto man helped me carry it up onto my patio and they lived there until mid-July when they outgrew it.

Until then I had a simple routine with the chickens. I'd wake up by 6:30 a.m. every day to feed them and give them water. I left an old bag underneath the cage to catch the poop that had fallen, not so much to protect the tiled patio as to collect it to fertilize my garden. Once a week I would be sure to give the inside of the cage a scrubbing to remove the poop that had accumulated on the boards. Once, I was cleaning the cage and one of the chickens escaped. It couldn't completely escape since the patio door was closed off but it kept running away from me. Luckily another volunteer was at my house at the time. We were able to corner it underneath the cage and put it back inside after its brief taste of freedom. Only one other time did any of the chickens try to escape the cage in the five weeks they resided there, and I was able to catch it and put it back in before it even got a full three seconds of freedom. I wasn't as lucky with the enclosure, which one specific chicken escaped from regularly.

I surprised even myself with the construction of an outdoor enclosure for them. To save effort and to guard against thieves I chose to put it next to my back door. It was an ideal location since I used the two walls and the staircase on the third side to reduce my work. The chickens could go under the stairs in the rain meaning I didn't have to build a roof, and the completed three sides meant that I only had to build one fence. But making that one fence was not easy. Pa Thomas contributed by collecting the raffia bamboo wood that I used to construct it and by helping dig the three initial vertical pieces into the ground to create a semblance of structure. From there I had to complete the rest of the fence, almost entirely made of village materials. Pa Thomas found the raffia bamboo wood down by the stream while I used my machete to both cut and split the wood into beams instead of going out to buy a proper saw. After two days, including many times hitting my own fingers with the hammer, I had a three-foot high fence that I was proud of. I grabbed the chickens out of their cage and carried them upside down through my living room, then put them one by one into their new enclosure. They seemed to love their new enclosure right off the bat. They took dust baths by rubbing themselves into the dirt, content after having just spent over a month in a raised wooden cage. I kept a close eye on them that first day, and I'm glad I did. As the sun was setting they started getting antsy. I wasn't surprised by it because they acted the same way in their cage. However, I was surprised when one of the chickens jumped up and almost got to the top of the fence. A few minutes later I was even more surprised when one managed to jump up almost to the top, then used its claws to land on a lower beam before hooking its neck around the top level to climb its way up. I quickly and unceremoniously pushed it back into the enclosure before putting in another beam as it got darker and started to drizzle. The next day I went to market and asked Pierre how much higher I needed to make the fence. He said that they were just looking for something to roost on, and that if I built them one, they would stop escaping. I made them a simple two-level perch from my remaining raffia wood thinking that it would solve my problems.

Pierre was wrong about the escape attempts. Just a week later I was sitting in my living room when movement by my back door caught my eye. I looked up saw a chicken in my doorway. At first I thought that it was a bold village chicken. Then I quickly realized that it wasn't any random village chicken, it was my chicken. I was confused about how it got out until I tried to catch it. While trying to corral it against the outside of the fence, it scurried up the steps and through a gap in the railing, back into the enclosure. I then had to grab some rope to weave between each of the pillars of the railing in an attempt to guard from any more escape attempts. It turned into a battle between me and the chickens, or more specifically one chicken that I ended up naming Blaine since he kept magically appearing on the other side of the fence. Multiple times I came home to find him standing by my back steps not knowing how to get back in. I tore open a large bag to create a barrier; Blaine just jumped over it. I tore open a second one to make the barrier act more like a slanted ceiling. It took three days but eventually Blaine got over that one, too. Every time I thought I had it closed off, Blaine would find a new way to escape. Until I was able to close off the ceiling of bags completely, I ended up babysitting the back steps from 5:45 to 6:15 p.m. when they were most active. I would watch Blaine hop his way up to the second row of the roost, stretch his neck up, and take the leap.

There was a learning curve for both Blaine and me when it came to escaping and capturing. Every time I updated the enclosure, it would take a bit for him to figure out a path to freedom. At first, I was very good at catching him. I'd trap him against the fence since he didn't want to be too far from his friends, food, and water, and then grab him as he tried to sprint past me. One time he went up the stairs and I caught him mid-air as he tried to fly over me. But he soon learned my tricks. During one escape, over a week since his previous one, he refused to be herded towards the fence. He instead went up and down the hill hugging the bushes on the opposite side. I ran around the bushes back and forth for 20 minutes trying to get him to move out into the open. It only worked when I threw some food out on the ground next to the fence. I ended up corralling him into my house, closing the door behind me to block off the escape route, and chasing him around my living room before eventually catching him in my kitchen.

When I purchased my chickens, I planned on keeping them until I killed them for my party. Then, when someone told me they would be great gifts, I figured I would give them away right before I left. But then people came wanting to buy them. I was showing off some pictures while giving a training and a man asked if he could buy one of my roosters. He came at at the end of August. I figured I would keep the other five for the remaining two months. But I had told Pa Thomas that one of the chickens was for him as a thank you gift, and he took it to his concession at the beginning of September. Then, not even a week later one of his neighbors hiked three miles down the hills to check out the rest of my chickens. We struck a deal and the next morning he came back to give me the money for my four remaining chickens, put them in a crate, and attached the crate to his moto to take home. I was sad to see them go. I missed their wake up calls before 6:00 a.m. and their little chirps welcoming me home every day. My reaction to their sudden purchase validated my thoughts about having pets. If I almost cried about my chickens leaving, I would not have done well having to give up a cat or a dog.

While I greatly enjoyed my agriculture experience, I know that I was just a visitor. I farmed for barely two years. I had no dependents. If my chickens all died or if I had a bad harvest, there was no harm. My sunk costs were from my Peace Corps stipend, and I would get another stipend the next month. I wasn't planning on selling anything anyway. But for everyone around me, agriculture wasn't just what they did, it was how they survived. Anything they produced was either put on their table or sold to send children to school. This wasn't always accomplished. I never had to feel the sting of waking up to finding all of my pigs dead for the second year in a row as Angilbert once did. I never had to watch batch after batch of baby rabbits die and not know the cause. I never had to stress that the rains were over a month late wondering how my farm was going to produce enough food to feed both my family and my animals. I am aware of that but at the same time I don't let it take away from all that I was able to accomplish from an integrated farming perspective.

13

Even with everything that Cameroon threw at me, I was able to get up and get to work, at least most of the time. I had three main primary projects: my trainings, my grants, and my farm.

Trainings

While I loved doing my farm work, or at least seeing the results of it, the vast majority of my work was doing trainings and it is where I had the biggest results. Not many people saw my chickens or my garden, and only 15 people received the improved beans in the first round. In contrast, nearly 500 people attended at least one technical training, and many attendees reported using what they learned on their own farms. In that way, trainings had a much more measurable impact than my farm work did. I wasn't getting my hands dirty, and many times I felt like I was giving the same training over and over again, but my trainings were a big part of what I was able to bring to the people of Baleveng.

Before I could get started on doing trainings I needed to do a community needs assessment. In other words, I needed to talk with members of my community to learn what their needs were. To get from their needs to what I would do trainings on, I needed to do a quick analysis to find the intersection of their needs and wants, and my skills. Doing a community needs assessment was very difficult for me at first. While Angilbert turned out to be a great work partner, we got off to a slow start. After protocol was finished, he was not helpful in introducing me to others and I felt like he wanted me to be his volunteer and his volunteer only. He even said as much to me a few months into my service when he was upset that there were others in Banza and Baleveng who knew me and what I was doing there. But I couldn't do a community needs assessment based off of one person. On my daily walks early in my service I would be sure to talk about their farming needs whenever I stopped to chat with somebody. What I learned was that there were three major needs areas: soil nutrition, human nutrition, and food security. The soil was terrible after years and years of farmers using it and therefore the production was not as high as it could be. People also weren't getting their proper nutrients and lacked food security because they were only growing the cash crops of corn and beans.

At first, I tried attacking all of these issues with one solution: housing animals. To me it is a simple solution, and one that I did end up trying to demonstrate with my chickens. When the animals are housed, the farmers can collect the manure and use it on their farms, thus improving soil nutrition. If people house their animals then they have more control over reproduction and size because housed animals are generally better fed and get bigger. Additionally, by housing their animals, farmers are better protecting them from diseases. The animals are therefore happier, healthier, and bigger, which usually leads to improved reproduction rates. People actually laughed in my face when I made the suggestion to house their animals instead of letting them roam free. It was something that they had never done, and something that they never wanted to do. I could work my tail off trying to promote the idea of housing animals, but they were never going to adopt the practice. This is a perfect example of why the wants of the villagers are incorporated into the analysis of the community needs assessment. If people don't want to do something, you can't force them into it no matter how helpful you may think it will be.

At that time, I was also figuring out how to overcome the stereotype of being a source of money, which is something I fought throughout my time in Cameroon. For those truly interested in working with me, it wasn't actually difficult since they saw the value in the trainings I was giving. When people asked me what I had for them I would say "knowledge" before telling them to come to a training to get some of it. Since so many people practiced Christianity, I would tell them the parable of teaching a man to fish, explaining that anything I gave them would last a day but they could improve their profits for life with the knowledge I could give them.

Even with these struggles, I was able to adapt. I had to if I was going to get anything accomplished and I couldn't see myself spending two years in a country when my goal was to help people and instead not get anything done. Not everybody had that goal and that is okay. But for me, I constantly felt like I needed to be doing something if I was sacrificing by being far away from home and those that I loved. I focused on giving practical trainings. Instead of trying to attack everything in one training, I chose to work on what I deemed the biggest needs. Based on my conversations with those around me, it was clear that the priorities were the poor soil nutrition and a lack of food security. It is thanks to the Peace Corps I actually had the ability to address these issues. I was taught how to do a regular compost pile as well as a Japanese rapid compost called bokashi, both of which I passed on in ten separate training sessions. I loved these trainings. It was where people were the most enthusiastic, and it was a simple enough skill that I was confident in showing it. At the same time, it was one of my most successful trainings. Almost 300 people attended one of these trainings. By the end of my service, people were applying the bokashi compost to over six acres of land and seeing some amazing results. I'll never forget the day I was struggling up the last hill to the market when Tsague Caroline, one of the students at the agriculture school, stopped me. She immediately pulled giant carrots out of her bag to show me the results of the bokashi that she had applied to her garden. I had never seen carrots that big before, and I likely never will again.

The success of the trainings was due in part to the students at the local agriculture school like Caroline. The Ecole Familiale d'Agricole, or EFA as it was known, was the first place I did any of my numerous trainings. Thanks to Kenfack Paul, I was able to have a meeting with the staff at the school and they agreed to have me come visit each month to give trainings on different topics. Paul was someone who I considered a counterpart for the greater Baleveng area, a selfless hard worker who was always finding me new groups to have trainings with. Unlike in my work as a teacher that would start many months later, I was training adults who had at least graduated from the equivalent of high school. The enthusiasm was immediate during my first training in April 2018. The students asked tons of questions, which at that point were directed to Paul instead of to me. But I didn't mind. It was my first feeling of success after struggling for over three months at site.

In that one day I finally felt like I was going to be able to accomplish something. From that point, I jumped in. Any time Paul brought up another group that we could give trainings to, I accepted. Additionally, I asked the students at EFA to bring this knowledge to their quarters and villages, even offering to go to their villages to lend a hand with the trainings. Djmeli Vanel and Ngoufack Victor both took me up on my offer, leading to even more people getting trained. Whenever people asked me to come do trainings, I said yes. I felt that knowledge transfer was the best way to create sustainable projects, because it created a network of experts for others to reach out to long after I left Baleveng. For example, even while I was still in the village, people would ask other farmers who had applied the bokashi compost how to do it instead of me.

I ended up having regular trainings with five different groups. I taught over 60 women the nutritional benefits of soy and how to make both soy milk and tofu for their families, since while soy did not grow well on our farms, it was readily available at the market. I taught nearly 200 people how to cultivate mushrooms in practical trainings where many people paid for spawn in advance and brought home their inoculated substrate bags. Over 4,000 avocado trees were planted because of my tree grafting trainings. All three of these improved home nutrition while the latter two also improved food security by diversifying people's farming enterprises.

One of my most successful trainings was at the high school where my site mates taught. Ngnintezem Pierre, the principal who had gotten to know of me when I helped out with my site mates' clubs, had invited me to teach his students how to grow mushrooms and wanted to use an empty storage room as a model mushroom hut that others in village could look at and learn from. In my first training, I had over fifty students watching and participating as we made substrate, sterilized it, and mixed in mushroom spawn. Including subsequent trainings at the same school, over 125 students were trained in mushroom cultivation, and the model hut led to two more groups asking me to teach them as well. One of the back cover photos of this book shows what it was like to be surrounded by so many students while trying to explain and demonstrate how to create substrate from corn cobs.

I wish I could say that all of my trainings went as successfully. There were times when people would show up late, unprepared, or both. One of my mushroom trainings started four hours late because not only did all of the participants show up two hours late, but it also took another two hours to crush the corn cobs since they failed to do it in advance. My second mushroom training with the local high school started two hours late because they didn't bring a basin to mix the substrate, and we ended up mixing in the spawn by phone flashlight since the sun had set during the two-hour sterilizing process.

There were times when I offered to do trainings, such as offering to do a rabbit training with one of my groups and when offering Victor to do grafting trainings in his village, that they would flat out say no. But that's okay. I would rather have offered to give a training than for them to wish I had and I didn't. I would follow up with some people and ask them if they used the knowledge that I shared with them and oftentimes they'd say no. I would try to ask why not to figure out what their barriers to use were but sometimes there simply weren't any. Some people just wouldn't use the knowledge that I shared, and that's okay. I couldn't let these losses force me to forget the successes I was having.

There were even a few times when people asked me to do a training, and then didn't show up to it. At the first annual Banza village meeting I attended, several people asked me to give a tree grafting training. I got their contact information from them and then called them a week before the training. I then called them the day before to remind them. Not a single one showed up, which was tough for me since it was the Fourth of July and I was very homesick that day. It happens, and the only thing that you can tell yourself is that you did everything you could.

In a weird way, it was easier to appreciate those wins when I was getting the losses. One week, seven out of the nine things that I had planned were cancelled. As I mentioned, people were sometimes hours late if they did show up. This was difficult for me. While I was growing up, my dad instilled in me the importance of showing up on time, saying that if you show up late you are telling the other person that your time is more valuable than theirs. I was taught that it was disrespectful to be late. But that simply isn't true in Baleveng. Being late, or not showing up without saying anything, is not a no-no. I was not the first volunteer to struggle with this concept, and I won't be the last. But even when I knew that it is culturally acceptable to be late, there were times when I got frustrated, especially when I was waiting for trainings that people had requested. I felt disrespected when that happened, since after all it was something that they asked me to do. It took some time to remember that it wasn't about me. Things come up, people forget the time, and the rains fall. I cannot control any of that, in Cameroon or anywhere else. I would just have to try again, and I did and I got successes out of it.

Despite all of the barriers, I was able to train many people in ways that would allow them to improve their farm production, even though I didn't speak more than ten words of the local dialect, Yemba. Everybody would tell me how easy Yemba is, and I did give it an effort. I even paid to copy a book to learn it. But the only way to learn Yemba is to learn it from French. It is also a language with no tenses and it has many homonyms. I knew pretty early on that while I would be able to learn some conversational Yemba, I would never be able to give a full training in it. But there were many people in Banza and Baleveng, usually older adults, who did not know French. I had to be able to adapt to their lack of French knowledge, even as mine was steadily improving, and any illiteracy by others. Luckily for me, Paul was always willing to serve as a French-to-Yemba translator and if he wasn't there I could always ask for a volunteer. As for my flipchart paper, I remembered something I learned from when I was a sailing instructor at the Cotuit Mosquito Yacht Club. That was to teach to all three learning types: auditory, visual, and kinesthetic. I used a combination of strategies to reach each type of learner. I had the above-mentioned translators to help those auditory learners who did not know French. I used pictures whenever possible on my flipchart paper to help with both the language barrier and illiteracy as well as to focus on any visual learners. Finally, I would always try to incorporate a practical portion to the training. That could be mixing compost or organic pesticides or grafting trees. Some people simply learn better by doing, which I found to be a large portion of those I taught. Many didn't feel confident enough to do it themselves unless they had done it with supervision, or at least seen it done before. I would get them to do as much as possible to give them a feel for it.

Grants

It was while my trainings were just getting off of the ground that the other project that helped defined my service was started. That project was the Pisciculture Training Center. It took two separate grants and spanned 18 months of my service. While in my other work I was going out to different parts of Baleveng to give trainings, with a completed Pisciculture Training Center people from all over our village, and even the West region, could come to our center to learn almost every facet of fish farming.

It started in March of 2018 when I was at my In-Service Training in Ebolowa, the same city we visited during our first few days in Cameroon. During the second week, our program managers told us that they had extended the deadline for model farmer grant applications. The money was from the USAID West African Food Security Partnership, and it was slated to go towards model farmers who worked with the Peace Corps to both improve their practices and serve as examples to teach those around them. I had originally not applied to the grant since I had only been at site for three months, and I had only just found a new work partner in Paul. I did not want to bring up this opportunity for him because I didn't want him to misinterpret it as free money towards any project he wanted.

The third and final week of the training included our counterparts. Each volunteer and their counterpart presented their community needs assessment and their plans for the coming months, as well as giving feedback on the presentations of other duos. The rest of the week was devoted to making sure that both volunteers and counterparts understood specific aspects of our work, such as creating project plans and measuring results. During one of the coffee breaks, Paul turned to me and started telling me about his plan to expand his fish farming enterprise, to allow it to become a training center. A lightbulb went off in my head. Here he was, telling me about a long-term project idea that he was going to do, when just the week before I dismissed doing a grant because there was nothing in mind. I told him that there was an opportunity for me to be able to help with the project, and for that to happen I needed him to get cost estimates and draw a map of the intended project design within the following two weeks. We decided that we would break up the project into two phases, partly because of the sheer size of the project and partly because we would not be able to use the fish reproduction hut from the second phase until the fish we purchased with the first grant were at least a year old.

Our first phase, therefore, was to dig two fish ponds, using two different drainage methods. The two methods were to show visitors two different options that they could use for their own fish ponds. As a result, our first phase was a simple process that was approved relatively quickly. I was impatient to get the money to get started. I felt like I hadn't done much yet (it was before my first training at the agriculture school), and I knew that with this project I would see real time progress as I watched the two fish ponds being dug. I knew I would see the two different pond drainage systems as they were being constructed. I knew that I would be there the day that the fish went into the ponds. This was something I could show off as well. Paul and I could show people the two different drainage systems that were put in and they would be able to choose which one would work best for their own fish ponds in the future. I could (and did) take my family there when they came to visit. I could not do that for farms with bokashi or organic pesticides applied to them, since to the untrained eye they looked just like every other farm.

A few months after we completed the first grant, we knew it was time to prepare for phase two to complete the Pisciculture Training Center. This phase involved digging a water catchment system complete with a hollow cement block to collect it, building a mud brick hut that would be used to reproduce fish, digging a much smaller pond for the baby fish to live in until they were big enough to be introduced to the bigger pond environments, and constructing a fence around the ponds to protect the investment from thieves. The water catchment system and subsequent piping was used to provide the water to the mud brick hut for the reproduction process. The baby fish needed to stay in the small pond until big enough because otherwise they would be eaten by other fish. Given the scale of the project and the number of parts, the second grant was much more complicated from start to finish.

What did not help with this process were the numerous delays that we had before we even got the money. I loved working with Paul, but he waited until dry season had already started to give me the cost estimates and maps for the project I needed to start the application. I knew it would take a long time for us to get the money and had asked for the estimates many times during the previous months, hoping that we would be getting the money just as the three month long dry season started. Any construction is difficult at best once the rainy season arrived.

After that we got hampered by a delay of my own causing. There were signatures that we needed to get during the second grant that were not needed in the first. That was because rather than going through USAID via the project managers, our second project was going through the Peace Corps Partnership Project, the Peace Corps version of crowdfunding and therefore had to go through Peace Corps Headquarters. It sounds simple, and in theory it is, but there are many steps that I didn't even know the order to. These signatures were one of those steps. I was under the assumption that we needed these signatures for me to be allowed to submit the application. I waited until the next time I was heading through Yaoundé to get them. Only then, weeks later when I was finally there, did I learn otherwise. I asked the country director for her signature for my grant form and she asked me if it had been approved already. Needless to say, I was kicking myself for that error. I was still hoping that we would be able to get the money before the dry season had ended, but due to my own misunderstandings I knew in that moment that the rains would arrive in Baleveng before the money hit my bank account, assuming our request was even approved.

Then we were delayed simply because those in the office were swamped with work. Usually grant requests are looked at during the first week of the month, and I confirmed that by asking someone who had gotten theirs approved the month before. Since they were busy, it got pushed back by a few weeks. My grant was not looked at until a month after it was submitted, and while I was grateful that it was approved without any problems, I was again kicking myself for my initial delay. If I had not made the mistake with the signatures, I would have gotten my grant approved a full six weeks earlier.

Just when I thought I was in the clear, I got an email from Peace Corps Headquarters in Washington D.C. regarding the grant request. While the staff in Cameroon had no issues with the project, those at headquarters were unsure of its sustainability and how it would help others in the area. To me it was simple: knowledge is free and others can use that knowledge to dig their own fish ponds and reproduce their own fish. The main barrier was that people did not have the knowledge, and this pisciculture training center would give them that knowledge free of charge. I was confused and frustrated that it wasn't going through headquarters as efficiently as I wanted because I was following the exact same concept of the model farmer grant that we completed the year before without any problems. I was already not in a good place mentally since this was the same time was when I could barely walk after the second wart removal. I ended up having to go back and forth a few times with headquarters to better explain the project, which again was my fault for not having done well enough in the first place. But I was having difficulty accepting that after having already accepted the two most recent delays as my fault. It was mentally exhausting to work and reframe what I had written to appease those at headquarters, knowing that given the high volume of grant requests from around the globe it would take them a few days to look at it before sending it back again with more questions. During this time, I was angry overall with myself, and was questioning why I was even trying to accomplish the grant at all. I was about ready to give up on the grant request and tell Paul that we were denied when I finally got approval.

When doing a Peace Corps Partnership Project, however, approval does not mean the money will hit your account promptly. What it means is that those at headquarters have created your crowdfunding website for you. From that point, you still have to market your project and raise the money. It takes however long it takes to raise the money, and then a few weeks more for headquarters to go through it all and send the money to Cameroon before the Cameroon staff sends it to your bank account. It was at this point that I was lucky. First, I have a large network of loving family and friends who either donated to the project directly or shared the link to spread the word about the project. It took me only a few days to raise half of the money. I would check the webpage every chance I could to see how much money was left to raise, but after those first few days the fundraising stalled. One night I was doing this and the project had been taken down. I panicked. I had only raised half of the money at that point and was worried that they had found another issue with the project. Instead of emailing the grant coordinator of Peace Corps Cameroon, I directly emailed the woman at headquarters who I had been emailing back and forth with about my previous issues. Within the hour, I was told that my grant had been fully funded which was why the project was pulled from the website. An anonymous donor who regularly donates to Peace Corps had seen my project and called headquarters to tell them that he would be funding the rest of the project. If I wasn't already in bed my jaw would have hit the floor. The speed at which the grant was funded thanks to my family and friends and the anonymous donor made me forget all of my frustrations with my own stupidly caused delays. It felt like my luck had drastically changed and now that it was funded, I stopped doubting if the project was ever going to get done.

Eventually the money hit my account and we were able to start. It took longer because of the rains. Paul had to save up money to buy two tarps to protect the dried mud bricks from becoming just mud again in the rain. By the time the bricks were done, the soil under where he was planning on putting them to build the reproduction hut was bogged down from rainwater. The solution, which took a long time to figure out, was to construct the building from the top down. He built the roof first to protect the mud brick walls as they were being built up. We were also blessed by an unseasonal dry month that allowed the walls to be successfully built.

Our other problems were of our own causing. The first was that while we had talked about digging a small enclosure for the baby fish and had included it in our grant request narrative, we failed to account for it in our budget. Since our grant was contingent on giving at least one training before closing the project, we had to come up with a way to separate the baby fish from the adult fish that would otherwise eat them but keep them in the same pond. Paul came up with a simple solution, similar to a floating shark cage but instead of metal was a fabric that would let water pass through but not fish. This ended up being a tool we taught at the training center as an alternative for villagers who do not have the resources to dig a second fish pond. Our second challenge was that Paul's fish would not be mature enough to reproduce until long after I left. It is hard to do a practical training on fish reproduction without fish that can actually reproduce. The original plan was for Paul to go out and buy a male fish and two female fish so that we could do trainings while the rest of his fish continued to mature. However, his source for adult fish and hormones with which to reproduce them was in the North West region, one of the two Anglophone regions. While we were trying to do this, travel was only permitted there on the weekends because of the war between separatists and armed forces. Paul made an attempt and was stuck on a bus overnight, so we were forced to do a theoretical training and afterwards showed everyone who attended the property. The plan is for Paul to do practical trainings with the next volunteer to continue the work of the training center.

The project came down to the wire. It took over nine months from when Paul gave me the budget, but we were able to get it done before I left in November 2019. I later read advice from former volunteers against trying to start a grant of such magnitude when a volunteer has less than a full year left in their service. After dealing with the stress of timing and our delays, I understand that. But as my dad would regularly remind me, it didn't matter how long it took for the Pisciculture Training Center to be completed, no matter how much it stressed me out at the time. What mattered was that it got done. In the end, the project worked out.

14

Throughout my service, I was constantly being inspired by the work other volunteers were doing. It is actually what led me to become a teacher for a year, even though it wasn't what I had set out to do when I visited the school. Many fellow agriculture volunteers and health volunteers had started agriculture or health clubs at their nearby schools. As my first full year in Cameroon was drawing to a close, I was still looking to see what more I could do in Baleveng. The starting of the next school year was a great opportunity. I saw having a club with the College Evangelique de Baleveng as an opportunity to branch into working with the youth of the community, something I had yet to do. I went to meet with the Nono Pierre, the principal, in September 2018 to discuss starting an agriculture club similar to those that other volunteers had started. Somehow, I walked out of that meeting as a member of the staff. I became a health and environment teacher in charge of four levels: 6eme, 5eme,

4eme, and 2nd, the American school equivalent of 6th to 10th grades. Instead of the optional weekly agriculture club I walked into the meeting wanting, I was suddenly responsible for teaching 60 students, as young as 10 years old and as old as 20, divided into two separate groups that each met for two hours a week.

I was looking for an opportunity and I got one, even if I didn't think I was ready for it. I realized that agriculture work ties in well with both the health and environment subjects and thus tried to create my course with an agriculture focus. That was about the only advantage I had in doing this class as someone whose prior teaching experience was limited to teaching 8 to 12 year olds how to sail for a few summers.

On my first day for each group I did a quick session with them going over the plan for the year, getting their input on what they wanted to learn, and trying to learn their names. I thought that if I built a rapport with them off the bat and also got their input on what they wanted to learn, they would be at least somewhat invested in the class and more likely to pay attention. I was wrong. During the first month, the students were testing the new white teacher, and I was failing. Part of that was because most schools in Cameroon follow the corporal punishment system. I didn't want to report them for their terrible behavior because I didn't know what would happen to them, and whatever it might be, I didn't want to be responsible for it. I had seen students at a local primary school getting hit for being late and being berated for crying while it happened. There was even a discipline master at most schools who was in charge of punishments. The kids found out pretty quickly that I wouldn't be hitting them myself or even reporting them, and any respect they had been giving me went out the window. Once, they all got up halfway through class and simply walked out the door, ignoring me and the class schedule. I was their last class for the day and they just went home. By the time the first exam rolled around, half of the students from each group stopped showing up, realizing that since their "mandatory" class wasn't on their report cards, their attendance didn't actually matter.

For a long time, I thought that I was the problem and that the students respected their other teachers, but I eventually learned that it wasn't just me. It was an exam day and I was handing out the test when Junior, one of my students, rushed in late. The censor of the school was right behind him. She demanded that he give her the hat he was wearing, since wearing hats on school grounds is not permitted. Students can wear hats up to the gate but once they step foot on school grounds the hat must be in their bag. I have seen the censor ask for hats before, and usually she puts it in her office for safe keeping to ensure that the students do not put it back on their heads when she isn't looking. These students got their hats back at the end of the school day. Junior, however, refused to give her the hat and instead made the censor chase him around the classroom. While this was happening, the other students told him that he should just give up his new prized possession since he would just get it back later. The hat wasn't worth getting a 0 on the exam, since if he did not give up the hat he would not be allowed to sit for the test. He fled the room and the censor left shortly after.

Ten minutes later, Junior tried to sneak back into the room with the hat on his head. Before he could even ask for a copy of the exam the censor walked into the room once again demanding his hat. The other students continued to tell Junior how dumb they thought it was that he was willing to get a 0 over this, telling him again that he would get the hat back at the end of the day. He finally gave up the hat, but the other students were wrong. By that time, he had disrespected the censor to the point of embarrassment. As punishment for the complete lack of respect that Junior showed her, she stood directly in front of him as she tore his hat in two with just her hands. My jaw fell. A different student, Becker, caught my reaction and giggled into her hand. I could not believe how the censor manhandled the ball cap. I felt badly for Junior but in such a strict punishment system it wasn't smart for him to test the censor like that. I also couldn't believe that Junior, or any student, would disrespect the censor. I understood when the students tested me and disrespected me knowing they'd likely get away with it, but to disrespect someone who is part of the school administration was completely different. Finally, I was grateful that Junior wasn't beaten for his actions.

In my initial meeting with the Pierre, he asked me to start a school garden with my students. Every week for two months I asked them to bring their hoes and machetes to start this project. I asked other staff members to help remind them. Pierre loved the project idea but not even he could get the students to bring their farm materials to class. I once offered extra credit to those who brought their farm materials. The next week just one girl brought a machete. Eventually halfway through November enough students in the 6eme/5eme class brought their materials to clear land, create garden beds and plant carrots. Since it was already dry season by that time, they had to water the garden a few times a week, even during the Christmas holiday. Some students were devoted to the garden, and were excited to eventually eat the fruits of their labor, but they never got the opportunity. After all of the work my students put in to keep the garden alive, other students at the school stole the carrots before we harvested them. It was one of those situations that could not have been prevented and there was nothing that could be done. I tried to tell to the students the benefit of at least having the knowledge for how to properly grow carrots that they could take to their own home gardens. But it wasn't the same for that group of disappointed 10 to 14 year olds, and I couldn't blame them.

These were some of the struggles that I faced when the students showed up, but there were too many times to count that I showed up at the school after hiking three miles to get there and there were no students around. Sometimes, there were other events scheduled that I had no idea about, such as fitness testing day for all of the schools in Baleveng. Another time I showed up on multicultural day. It was the foreign language teacher's idea to have the students prepare dishes from the home country of the foreign language they were studying (either Spanish or German) and present it in that language. They then had to answer questions in the foreign language from different teachers about the dishes. I had never heard of such an activity happening at one of the local schools, and I thoroughly enjoyed getting to watch and eat. One of the German speaking groups brought in a long sausage roll with some bread and called it a day, but most of the other groups put some serious effort into the meals they presented. I couldn't be upset that there wasn't class when it was for a different academic endeavor. But it was frustrating during the times when there simply wasn't school that day and I wasn't notified, such as a week before the Christmas holiday was supposed to start or when there was still a month left of class on the academic calendar and I was told that classes were done for the year.

Most of the time, however, it was the result of students simply leaving for the day before my class started. I started showing up earlier, thinking that maybe they didn't know I was coming even though we were supposed to have class at the same time every week. When I would go inside the teachers' lounge to study for the LSAT, they would sneak out the gate. I would head down to the classroom to find it empty, even though I had seen my students earlier in the day. I wouldn't let myself get upset because there was only so much I could do. It was the students' choice to skip out. If they didn't want to learn about how organic fertilizers can make a difference to both human and environmental health then who was I to force them to stay? I knew I wasn't the only teacher at the school stuck with the issue because they weren't staying for their other classes either, and other teachers would complain about it.

Through all of the challenges, I did enjoy moments of teaching. Any time it rained, sometimes loud enough to drown out my voice, students would yell out, "Madame, it's raining!" like when students in the United States say that it's snowing. In both, students hope for an early dismissal. The roads to my students' homes, as the road to mine, would get muddy and difficult to pass. But I knew as well as they did that once it had already started raining that it was too late. If I were to let them go they would have just stood under the roof outside of the classroom door because nobody walks in the rain except for the crazy white girl.

I also enjoyed the challenge of teaching in a second language. Sometimes my students didn't have the base knowledge I assumed they did and I would have to come up with definitions in French on the spot to bridge the gap. This included a lot of miming, like when I told them that the nervous system was a system of roads from the brain telling the rest of the body what to do. I pointed at my head telling them that the brain created the message, then pointed down the unseen route of the nerves that the message travelled down to my leg which I then moved slowly forward after it received the message. Many times they would correct my pronunciation. One student, Ymelda, corrected me on how I would say "aujourd'hui" (today) almost weekly while I was telling them what they would be learning that day. Other times students would come to the board and ask for the chalk to make a correction to my spelling. While these corrections took away time from the lesson, I encouraged them. If they were correcting me then they were paying attention. It also encouraged them to practice their listening and reading skills. I didn't purposefully mispronounce or misspell anything to do this, but I saw it as an unexpected benefit for the students who showed up to class.

The last thing that I did with the students was plant moringa trees all around the campus. I was in the middle of a moringa seed distribution and the principal wanted trees planted on school grounds. As the trees grew, students would be able to use the tree leaves to improve their nutrition by turning them into a powder and putting it into their food. The trees would also provide seed pods that the students could take home in order to plant the trees at their own homes. This would provide their families with the same nutrition. These seeds also can be used to filter water, which would help counter the problem of drinking dirty water. Unfortunately we had bad luck for our planting. It was well after the start of rainy season, but the rains weren't as consistent as they were the year before. None of the trees we planted sprouted even a little bit because they didn't get enough water during the critical time right after planting. But at least the students learned general information about the trees' value and how to plant them.

I would like to think I left a positive impact on the students, or at least I hope they learned a thing or two. While they may not have always behaved well in the classroom, they always made time to say hello to me when they saw me outside of the school. Even if I wasn't having the best day I would always appreciate the smile on their face when they said hello or when they would enthusiastically introduce Madame Leigh to whomever they were with. It was bittersweet that day when they told me classes were over a month earlier than I expected. I was relieved because it meant that one of the harder projects I tried during service as completed. But at the same time I was disappointed. I felt that I was only just connecting with the students, like Franky and Nelly who were enthusiastically answering my questions about malaria on what ended up being our last day in the classroom. I also knew that I wouldn't be teaching them the next year since I would only be around for a small part of the following school year.

15

I greatly enjoyed the ups and downs of my work, learning about the Bamiléké culture, and trying to survive my Peace Corps service. My absolute favorite part, however, was when my sister Casey and my dad, the people with whom I talked the most, were able to see for themselves what my life was like. They could connect what I had told them with what they were experiencing. Their experiences have helped them have a better understanding of what my life was like. I will forever be grateful for them for wanting to spend the entire week that they had in Cameroon in Baleveng. And while they both admit that they could never really understand my life there since they were only there for a week instead of over two years, they got a much better understanding than anyone else really could.

Their visit was an adventure, basically from the moment they landed in Yaoundé until they got back on the plane heading to Boston. I picked them up from the airport with the most trusted taxi driver likely in Peace Corps Cameroon history, Lamerenjoya Abdou, and he dropped us off at a hotel for the night before helping us get to the bus station the following morning. Abdou truly cares about all Peace Corps Volunteers in Cameroon, even the ones he doesn't know. When I was leaving at the airport for my first vacation he walked me inside to make sure that I knew what I was doing before he got back in his car to return to the city. When dropping my family and me off at a Yaoundé hotel, he mentioned that since we were trying to make the long voyage to the West region on a Friday, we should leave the hotel at 6:00 a.m. because everybody would be heading back for another weekend of funerals. I did agree with him with the reasoning for leaving at that time, but after seeing how exhausted my family was after their long travel day and remembering how long mine felt when I first arrived there, I asked him to pick us up at 6:30 a.m. instead, which ended up being a mistake. We got to the bus station at close to 7:00 a.m., and there was a giant crowd of people waiting for a bus that wasn't yet there. We tried driving to another station that had a bus and not as many people, with the baggage man telling us that they went to Bafoussam.

We said goodbye to Abdou, thanking him for all of his help and saying that we would see him next week to take my family back to the airport, and got in the ticket line to patiently wait our turn. When we finally got to the front of the line we were told that the bus actually didn't go to Bafoussam and instead went to a completely different city in the West region. We left that agency and walked back to the one we had originally stopped at. Luckily buses going to the same areas of the country leave from the same areas of Yaoundé. Directly outside the agency we first stopped at, which was even more crowded and still missing a bus, was a different bus. Not all buses are run by agencies. Some are buses that go back and forth between cities and allow people to get on and off at will. I decided that we would take the non-affiliated bus because there were more people waiting at the agency than there would be available seats on the bus whenever it arrived. While we were boarding, people tried to pickpocket both Casey and my dad, but luckily they had followed my advice of zipper pants pockets. We got on board, I threw my bag under the seat in front of me and told my family to choose open seats next to windows. I paid the man who was asking for our money for the tickets and sat down to wait. Ten minutes later a man asked me to pay for our tickets, with blank ones in his hand. It turns out that even though I had been living in Cameroon for 15 months, I still hadn't mastered everything. Apparently, I had paid someone who was pretending to be working with the bus. I saw the man outside and yelled at him over Casey through the open window, in French, that he was a thief and that he needed to give me my money back. He only gave me some of it back, claiming that was all that I had given him. I usually carry just enough money for the voyage plus a little bit of emergency money, but since the bus was the most expensive part of our journey, I didn't have enough money to pay for all of us twice. I continued to yell at the man as Casey and my dad stared at me in shock. Casey broke out in hives from anxiety, and I couldn't blame her. She and my dad got thrown into the thick of things right away while when I arrived there I had had time to slowly acclimate to these aspects of life. I hate admitting this and have tried very hard to forget it but we ended up having to pay them some American money since the man with the rest of my money simply ran away.

We had to sit on opposite sides of the bus, since there were no seats left in the column that my family had chosen, while we waited for it to fill. Meanwhile I stewed about what just happened and silently stressed because I used the rest of my CFA to pay the actual ticket man before we resorted to some American money. As usual for transportation, we waited for the bus to fill in order leave. When boarding, I assumed that it would fill quickly given the high number of people waiting at the bus station. But I later realized that all of those travelers had purchased their tickets already— they were not going to lose that money to get to Bafoussam any faster. After all, they weren't in any rush since the funerals start late Friday afternoon. The last few people for the bus trickled on which, as always, felt like it took forever. We had filled out my row when a woman got on with her baby to complete my dad's row. Then the baby started wailing. The mama ended up getting off of the bus, and as soon as they got off the bus the baby stopped crying. Apparently it was afraid of the white people, and the mama chose to not get back on. While we did have to wait even longer for the mama's place to be filled before the bus could leave, I suppose I should be grateful that we didn't have to deal with a crying baby for the long bus ride.

Eventually, we made it to Bafoussam. I wasn't sure that we were going to. I'm pretty sure my dad didn't think so either. He realized after it was too late to change seats that he made the mistake of was sitting on the wheel-well, which was my fault but meant that he was stuck with zero leg room, with one bag under his feet and one in his chest on top of his raised knees. While he was dealing with that, I stressed for nearly the entire bus ride to Bafoussam about whether we would make it there in time for me to be able to take more money out. After five hours on the bus, he got relief and I finally accepted that there was nothing that I could do about the money until we got to Bafoussam. We stopped on the side of the road as a bathroom break, which meant that Casey and my dad witnessed me and a bunch of Cameroonian ladies squatting down to pee. It was definitely not a part of their expectations for the trip, but I learned to take every bathroom opportunity on those travel days. Back on the bus, I forced my dad to take my seat, where he was at least able to put one bag completely on the floor while I took the wheel-well seat behind Casey. A few hours later we made it to Bafoussam, where I rushed to drop my family off at a restaurant to order us some food for a very late lunch while I literally ran away to take some money out. Almost all volunteers in Cameroon use yellow or orange money huts to take their money out. Affiliated with the major phone companies of MTN and Orange respectively, these huts allow you to make withdrawals from your mobile money account on your phone that is connected to your bank account. Instead of waiting in line at the one branch of my bank in Bafoussam, I pulled money from my bank digitally to my mobile money account and went to one of the hundreds of huts scattered around the city to get the cash quickly.

We did eventually get to Baleveng, about 12 hours after leaving the hotel. When we finally got there, Kenfack Paul insisted on meeting us at the market. I called him while en route and he met us there right when our bus stopped for us to get out. I couldn't help but feel both excited and nervous about their first glimpses of Baleveng, which I considered home. I think they felt the same way, the nerves hitting likely when they realized that we would have to ride motos to my concession. Paul, a father figure to me, brought my dad, while Casey and I grabbed rides from drivers I've used before. At first, my driver kept us in the back of the pack, giving me space to take videos of them. I will forever have videos of them riding their motos with their baseball hats backwards, buffs over their mouths to guard against the dust, and grasping on the luggage rack on the back of the moto like I did on my first ride in Banganté. When we arrived, Paul stayed behind to talk with us a little bit. He has a relatively good grasp of English which he used to make sure my dad understood him. He said that my dad shouldn't worry about my safety because he looks over me, that I am his American daughter and he is my Cameroon father. He told my dad that he should be proud of what I have done in Baleveng and that I work hard. I am not someone who needs validation for the work that I do. Even so, it was touching that Paul took the time to tell my dad all of that. Later when I thanked him, he said that he was only telling the truth.

Other than that first conversation with Paul, I served as a translator for Casey and my dad, the difficulty of which I didn't realize until I was committed to doing it. To me it felt as if I was slowing down the conversation by translating it back and forth, and since I had to translate before I could even respond, it was as if I wasn't an active participant in those conversations unless it was a side comment in one language or the other that wasn't getting translated. Usually these conversations would be for just a few minutes but one evening Paul and his wife Charlotte came to visit as one of my families visiting the other. I served as the translator for over an hour. While Paul knows English, Charlotte does not and it would have been rude to have a conversation completely in English when she took the time out of her day to visit and bring a thoughtful gift in the form of a huge bag of potatoes for us to eat throughout the week.

The week that Casey and my dad visited was spent seeing the most important parts of my life there. We went to see Paul's fish ponds, in between the two phases of the Pisciculture Training Center. I took them to watch me teach at the College Evangelique de Baleveng. We toured my model plot. We visited Angilbert to see some of his farm plots and animal enclosures, and he showed them how raffia palm wine is tapped. Angilbert told us to choose an afternoon to return and pick up a rabbit to eat. We asked him to help us skin the rabbit, which we did it at his house. He tied the rabbit up to a post, killed it by knocking it unconscious with the handle of a machete before cutting its neck, and then peeled the skin off of the rabbit from the feet down to the head with a small razor blade. He then put it into a bag for us to carry home and cook. It was the first time either Casey or my dad saw an animal that they were about to eat get killed, and I wasn't sure how they were going to react. I was mentally prepared for what was ahead since I had already killed a few chickens myself and had witnessed the process for the rabbit before, but I wasn't sure what to expect with Casey or my dad. Surprising me, Casey jumped in on wanting to butcher the rabbit and make rabbit stew with some of Charlotte's potatoes and carrots from the market.

We went to my market day twice, which as I've mentioned was something to look forward to every four days. After promenading them around the entire market, introducing them to everyone, and buying some food for the week on the first market day, we picked out a teal pagne with dark yellow and black flowers and visited my tailor to get matching shirts made. We picked them up the next market day along with the traditional hats that Paul's sister made for them. Both times we stopped at Sidonie, Veronique, and Gisele's restaurant for some spaghetti omelettes. Usually people get café au lait with it, which is a mug of some condensed milk and hot water with the option of either instant coffee or chocolate powder mixed in. While I came to think it was too much sugar, my dad loved the café au lait and compared it to a latte.

It wouldn't have been a trip to see the things that were a huge part of my life in Cameroon if we did not go see Dschang. Dschang is where I went to to pick up a package, get some Maggi arome sauce, orange juice, or other things not available at the Baleveng market, or do banking. It's also where I went when I just wanted a nice steak lunch, available at a restaurant that has a patio that overlooks Lake Dschang. We checked out the cultural museum right next door as well before seeing the rest of the town. I introduced them to my friends at the post office, the grocery store, and the artisanal market the city is known for. Afterwards, we caught one of the many cars that go back and forth between Baleveng and Dschang. I laughed to myself when we got in, knowing that while I was used to being in old, run-down cars packed with people, it was a new experience for my family. It ended up being the most run down car I ever had gotten a ride from in Cameroon. The motor wouldn't catch unless the front tires were turned all of the way to the right, there were only holes where there should have been taillights, and the front windshield was cracked like those of most bush taxis. We joked about whether the car was going to make it back to my village since it seemed ready to just give out every time we went up a hill. The driver would use the momentum of the previous downhill to get most of the way up the next one before the car had to do any work. After one downhill, we regretted our jokes as a passenger got out at the bottom on the left-hand side of the road and the car lost all of its momentum. Usually the driver goes back on the right-hand side of the road before climbing the hill but our driver didn't. He stayed on the left-hand side of the road as the car chugged up the hill, eventually dying halfway up. He then tried to push the car back down the hill a bit and jump in to kickstart the engine. When that failed, he put on the brakes so he could run up the hill to a boutique selling water bottles full of gasoline to dump into the tank. The car still wouldn't start. During all of this time, cars were whipping past us since we were still on the wrong side of the road. Eventually the driver got some help to push the car all of the way back down to the bottom of the hill and onto the side road the woman had gotten out on. There he was finally able to get the car started and up and over the hill on the correct side of the road; by some miracle the car ended up making its way all of the way to Baleveng.

Every night after dinner we would stay up playing cards and chatting. It was difficult to come back to an empty apartment after that knowing that it would be another 10 months before I was going to do that with them again. Given everything that we did, it may seem strange that it was one of my favorite parts of their visit. The sun is up from 6:30 a.m. to 6:30 p.m. in Cameroon, and as it got closer to sunset I would have to close my metal doors and windows to protect myself from the mosquitos. Combined with the terrible lights I had in my apartment, the end result was dark and lonely. I loved being able to spend those evening hours with people I love, doing something that at home we do regularly when we are all together.

All too quickly, my family's visit came to an end. We decided to break up the trip back to Yaoundé into two days to avoid repeating of the fiasco trying to get to village. The morning that we were leaving was the only morning available to properly greet the King of Baleveng. We were told that we would be having coffee, which was perfect for our travel plans. We showed up with all of our bags, since it didn't make sense to go all of the way back up to my house just to come back down to the market area again. The King realized we were traveling that day, and as the gracious host that he always is decided that coffee was not going to give us enough energy for our trip. Instead he provided us with a very early and classic lunch of plantains and chicken with beer. The food was great, as it always was whenever I visited the King. It was a good opportunity for my family to eat another classic Cameroonian dish because my cooking skills didn't allow for me to make any for them. My family was initially confused when they saw me take the beer at 9:00 a.m., but realized the rudeness of turning it down. While I usually don't drink, it was not my place to ask for soda or water because it was not offered. I'm pretty sure any time Casey talks about her visit, she brings up having beers with the King at 9:00 a.m. as the first time the two of us had one together.

While we ate, the King played a long video on his television from the village ceremony that happens once every three years so my family could learn a little bit more about his culture. I'm glad we were shown the video because my two years in village were in between two of the ceremonies. While watching the video we struggled to eat all of the plantains put in front of us, knowing that I could talk our way out of finishing the chicken but not both dishes. Casey tapped out after just two plantains, leaving my dad and I to struggle in an attempt to not be rude. When we went to take our leave with full stomachs, the King went to his private living quarters to get a gift for my dad as a thank you for the small gift they brought him. I was not expecting the giant wooden carving that he came back to his salon with. He told us that the five different scenes on the carving represented the different aspects of Bamiléké culture as he presented it to my dad.

That carving is safely in my dad's house in Massachusetts, but it took some effort to get it home. Getting it to Yaoundé was relatively easy, but apparently getting it back to the United States was a lot more difficult for them. I did not take them to the airport myself since I didn't think I would be much help. Instead I said goodbye to them at the hotel and had Abdou drop them off. They got harassed before even arriving at check-in by people who wanted to have them wrap the carving for protection. It is easy enough to ignore them but when you do need their services the negotiations can be fierce. The person who brought them to the wrapper wanted money along with the person who actually wrapped the carving. Luckily, my dad had followed my advice of separating the CFA bills I had given him into different pockets to avoid getting ripped off even more by people seeing just how much money he had on him.

With the carving safely wrapped, they checked in and went to go through security with all of their stuff. They carried everything onto the plane when coming to Cameroon, and planned on doing the same on the way back. The agents at security changed those plans, refusing to let my family take the carving or the wooden elephant bookends we purchased in Dschang onto the plane. They had to scramble to reorganize their bags to check the one with the bookends and check the wooden carving as a separate "bag" since it didn't fit in the hiking backpacks they were using. Someway, somehow, the carving and all of my family's things made it home even if when they finally got there they fell sick from food poisoning from airplane food. I can't help but laugh every time I think of how they were fine eating food that has given me amoebic dysentery but got food poisoning from the plane. I am also grateful for that timing, since it meant that we got to do everything that we wanted to do while they were in Cameroon.

I will always remember my family's visit, and that they wanted to see what my life was like. They could have wanted to go see some waterfalls or wanted to go to Kribi, the beach town in the South region. Instead, I got to do what I always do in village and got to showcase it. I ended up getting asked about how Casey and my dad were doing almost weekly until I left. After their visit I could talk with them about almost anything I was going through and they had a better understanding of what I was talking about. For example, I used to talk about the trip from Yaoundé to Baleveng, but after their 12 hour experience they understood how much of an effort it actually took. I could talk about a long day spent weeding at my model plot, and they would understand how large of a plot it was and how far away from my house it was. I could mention some of the people in village and they would be able to put a face to the name. And even though I have written this book to give people a better understanding of my life when they ask me, "How was Africa?," Casey and my dad have the most accurate understanding. Nobody will truly understand what my life was like specifically in village, but those two will be the closest simply by living it for a week. Other volunteers who also served in Cameroon or in other African countries will have a good understanding of the more general ways of life but Casey and my dad were some of the few who got to see what my life was like specific to Baleveng. For that I will always be grateful.

16

There is a defined period of time for the end of a Peace Corps service, between the Close of Service Conference two to three months before departure and the actual Close of Service date when the volunteer gets on a plane to return home. It is a time when work slows down as you prepare for it to be carried on without you, you say goodbyes, and you pack up to leave.

The Close of Service Conference is just what its name suggests. It is a time for all of the volunteers in a stage to get together one last time, to begin to learn about the processes and procedures of closing out a service. It was also a time to celebrate, held at the nicest hotel in Yaoundé. We were able to stuff our faces full of buffet food at every meal and swim in the pool when we weren't sitting in the conference room. It was when we divided ourselves up into three different departure groups. While we came to Cameroon together, it would not be feasible for all of us to leave at the same time. Those in the office have other work to do besides processing us out, so there can be a maximum of eleven people per departure group. There was something special about choosing our departure dates. It made our upcoming departure more real, since we finally knew when exactly we would be heading home.

Similar to the last night in Yaoundé during our first week in Cameroon, the last night of Close of Service Conference week included a dinner at the country director's house. The house was the same as it was when we first arrived, but other things had changed during the previous two years. At the first dinner we were a group of people who barely knew each other and had no idea what we were really getting into. This time, we were people who had come to know each other and had lived through our two years of service. Additionally, not all of us were there. Some volunteers had left during the two years, and a new country director had moved in early on in our service.

That dinner was one last time to celebrate together as a group all we had accomplished during our two years in Cameroon. After gorging ourselves for one last time before being sent to our sites again where we would have to fend for ourselves, there was an award ceremony. Ten volunteers (five health volunteers and five agriculture volunteers) were given small statues and certificates for awards of excellence. I am proud to be a recipient of a statue, and I will always look at it with pride knowing it is a symbol of appreciation from the Peace Corps for all that I had done.

By the time I got back to Baleveng, I had just ten weeks left before returning home for good. I planned out all of what I needed to do before leaving the village, and spread it out over those remaining weeks. The first part was completing my work, like finishing weeding my farm, and selling my chickens. My plan went completely out the window just three weeks into it when I became worried that a mole on my leg might be skin cancer. I lost a week preparing for and traveling to and from Yaoundé to have a biopsy done. When I got back to Baleveng, there were six weeks left until my departure date. I would not get the results for three weeks, but if positive I would likely be sent right home. As a result, I had to condense everything that I needed to do during six weeks into three, just in case my results came back positive.

During those three weeks, I took the time to prepare my things for an early departure. It was during this time that I learned that for security reasons (my village was too close to the Anglophone regions), my site would not receive a new volunteer once I left. So, I started to sell and give away the things that I had planned to leave for the next volunteer. Anything that I could live without for three weeks should my results not come back positive was sold or given away, including my couch, my extra mattress, and a ton of clothes that I did not plan to bring back to the United States with me.

I also made sure to explain to everyone what was going on. It was hard, telling them that I know that I was supposed to leave village on November 3rd, but I might have to leave three weeks early for treatment. My mindset was that I would rather tell everybody my personal business and say goodbye to them a few weeks early, than to not tell them anything and for them to feel slighted if I had to leave as soon as possible after getting my results. Some told me that they just knew it would be negative, others told me that God would not let me get skin cancer, and others told me they would pray for me. One woman told me that this was happening to me because I did not go to church. These conversations were difficult but they needed to be had.

It was for this reason that I made sure to schedule meetings with both the Chief of Banza and the King of Baleveng. I wanted to provide them with thank you gifts and letters before getting my results. My first meeting was with the Chief of Banza. I went there on a Sunday morning in my best pagne dress made of fabric with the blue pattern of the Bamiléké people. We sat and chatted for a bit, along with his wife and some other members of Banza. I gave him his gift of a nice bottle of wine, his letter, and the improved corn seeds that I reproduced on the land that he gave me. He then excused himself to go into a back room, and I assumed he was just putting the bottle of wine away. He came back out with a traditional hat — black, white, and red with little tufts sticking out in a circle around the head — and a traditional bracelet covered with the shells that symbolize Bamiléké royalty. He declared me Princess Leigh of Banza before putting these objects on me. He said that it was a thank you for all of the work that I had done in Banza, including the model farm, which many more people than I realized actually visited, and the mushroom work that I had started. He said that I will always be a daughter of the royal family of Banza, and that whenever I go back to visit I can stay at the royal palace.

Less than a week later, on the day that I was to receive my skin biopsy results, I had my meeting with the King of Baleveng. Similar to my meeting with the Chief of Banza, I simply wanted to give a gift and a thank you letter as a token of gratitude for all that he enabled me to do during my time in his village. Just a few hours earlier I got the relieving news of my biopsy results being negative for skin cancer, so it was already a great day. When the King arrived, we were led to a dining room that I had never been in before, instead of his living room that I had been to every other time I met with him. He had told me previously that he wanted to honor me, but I had no idea what it would be like. It was something I hope to never forget. When the King walked into the room, the other ten guests and I all stood and remained standing until he sat down. He started the meeting by telling us why we were all there. He said that the meeting and meal were to thank me for all of the hard work I had done for Baleveng. He talked about the bokashi organic fertilizer trainings I did, and how he believed it to be a great replacement for the chemical fertilizers that were causing diseases around village. He mentioned my tree grafting work as well.

After his introduction, the King told me to stand up and follow some of his wives out of the room. We went to the living room, where there was a bag of things waiting for me. The wives then took out the traditional items from the large bag and put them on me, one by one. First was a traditional vest, made of black velvet with intricate patterns sewn in with bright yellow, red, and green thread. They then put on me the traditional princess hat, very similar to the hat I received during my meeting with the Chief of Banza. This was followed by a long traditional necklace comprised of long white beads, short black beads, and short red beads. Finally, they put on a bracelet of very small white and black beads. I was finally ready to be led back to the dining room, where upon my entrance the King announced to everyone that I was officially Princess Leigh of Baleveng. The rest of the meeting was eating a nice meal and me giving him his gifts: a bottle of Jack Daniel's whiskey and his thank you letter.

During the same week of these meetings, I got another honor. Pa Thomas' grandson was named after me. There is now someone in Banza named Ndougni Thomas Leigh. You may think that this honor pales in comparison to both of my princess honors, but nothing could be further from the truth. Most villagers do not have the money for thank you gifts such as those the Chief and King gave me. Pa Thomas and his family wanted to make sure that their appreciation for the American member of their family was acknowledged nonetheless, and so they gave me the highest honor they could by naming their baby after me. For Thomas Leigh's entire life, his family can tell him and others about whom he was named after. By including my name in the newborn's name, they were telling me that they would make sure that I would not be forgotten after I left.

For the remaining few weeks in Baleveng, I simply appreciated everything. I knew that the day when I would get on a bus to Yaoundé and not be facing that long bus ride back was coming up quickly. I continued to say goodbye to people, not knowing when the next time I would see them might be. Instead of the party I had in mind when I bought my chickens, I had a small lunch of potatoes with tomato sauce, hard boiled eggs, peanuts, and lollipops for those in Banza who did the most for me. I toured the market and gave goodbye letters to my mamas who had looked out for me over the previous two years.

On one of my last days in Baleveng, I went to visit EFA, the agriculture school where I did so many trainings. I wanted to take the time to say goodbye to the people there, especially because my successful first training there gave me the confidence to keep giving training after training. While I was there I was presented with a peace tree to bring back with me to the United States. to plant. In traditional Bamiléké culture, the tree is meant to provide protection from evil spirits. The staff and students at EFA wanted to ensure that I would have peace and calm when I returned home to the United States.

In those last few weeks in Baleveng, I spent a lot of time thinking about all that the people of Banza and Baleveng had come to mean to me. Three emotions kept coming back up: honor, pride, and humility. Not everyone who had lived where I lived was thanked as much or honored as much as I was, and that was something that everyone made sure to remind me as they thanked me again and again. As I said my goodbyes, they forced me to acknowledge all of the hard work that I did and all of the positive impacts I made. I was humbled that the work that I did was even worthy of their thanks, when for two years I was just working.

One of these conversations in these last days almost broke my heart. I was talking with one of my mamas, and she was telling me about the impact that I had on her life during my short time in Baleveng. She said that the agriculture knowledge I shared allowed her to better support her ten children. She incorporated aspects of the several trainings I had given into her farm, both reducing her costs and improving her production. She housed her chickens, eliminating the cost of manure, and the bokashi organic fertilizer I taught her greatly improved her farm production. The orange-fleshed sweet potatoes I distributed, which I had viewed as a failure for so long, had greatly improved her home nutrition.

This conversation was one of the moments that I will always carry with me. I was sad about her situation and leaving her behind, wishing that I could do more. But I was also proud of all that I was able to do for her. When I joined the Peace Corps, my goal was to change the life of at least one person. Throughout my service it was difficult to keep away the nagging doubt that I was making any impact. Even after being named princess twice, I couldn't help but think at times that it was just because I was a white person trying to make a difference. But with one conversation all of those doubts went away. Just because I could not see the impact of all of the work that I was doing, it did not mean that the impact was not there.

As the bus was pulling away from Baleveng for the last time on November 3rd, 2019, I was understandably filled with emotions. I realized that the way of life that I had struggled through and had come to know and love was simply finished. There would be no more market days filled with spaghetti omelettes and great conversations. There would be no more happy laughter from people when I greeted them in Yemba. There would be no more muddy hikes or long days on the farm. My two years in Cameroon were the hardest years of my life, but joining the Peace Corps was the best decision I ever made. It was nothing like I imagined it when I accepted a business advising volunteer position in Peru. But as the bus was pulling away, I knew that I had had the best experience I possibly could, and that everything had indeed worked out.

Acknowledgements

There are many people who need to be thanked for all of their support for the last two years.

My family: My dad, Jim Dannhauser, my sister, Casey, my brothers Jim, Mike, and Rob, my sisters-in-law Caitlin and Dana, and future sister-in-law Maggie Lloyd.

Those who helped me directly with my book: Casey Dannhauser, Jim Dannhauser, Caroline Adelle Echols, and Maggie Lloyd.

To everyone who donated to the second grant project to complete the Pisciculture Training Center: Ali Carley, Jim Dannhauser, Jim & Caitlin Dannhauser, Rob & Dana Dannhauser, Steven & Beth Dannhauser, Kathy & Ron Livolsi, Maggie Lloyd & Mike Dannhauser, Liz Olsen, Kara & John Stamper, and the anonymous donor.

To everyone who wrote me letters or sent me care packages: Juhi Amin, Pam & Rich Boden, Paul Chatelain, Beth & Steven Dannhauser, Andrew Forney, William, Catherine & Sophie Hemmerdinger, Tyler Hyde, Sarah Williams, and Lauren Woodie.

Last but not least, to the staff at Peace Corps Cameroon. Thank you for all of your support, for keeping me healthy and safe, and for making everything that is in this book possible.

About the Author

Leigh Marie Dannhauser served in the Peace Corps as an agriculture volunteer in the West region of Cameroon from September 2017 to November 2019. She never saw herself becoming an author, but after journaling her experiences in Cameroon almost daily, she saw an opportunity to share her story with others and published *Nothing Works But Everything Works Out*, a memoir about her time in Cameroon, in December 2019. Born and raised in Bronxville, New York, Leigh has a B.A. in journalism and in religion from Washington & Lee University and M.S. in commerce from the University of Virginia. She is an aspiring human rights attorney and plans to start law school in August 2020. Leigh currently lives on Cape Cod.

Discussion Questions

- What was your initial reaction to the book?
- Did the book change your opinion or perspective about anything?
- What did you like or dislike? Why?
- What was your favorite passage?
- What did you know about the Peace Corps before reading this book?
- If you were a parent, would you want your child to serve in the Peace Corps? Why or why not?
- What aspects of the author's story could you most relate to? Have you ever had any similar experiences?
- What gaps do you wish the author had filled in? Were there points when she shared too much?
- If you got the chance to ask the author of this book one question, what would it be?

CPSIA information can be obtained
at www.ICGtesting.com
Printed in the USA
FFHW022012261119
56475848-62280FF